THE CULT
OF CRITICAL THEORY

By DM Schwartz, MD, MBA

ALSO BY DM SCHWARTZ:

Critical Race Theory, Ta-Nehisi Coates and his Book Between the World and Me.

An exploration of the meandering mediocrity in Ta-Nehisi Coates' award winning nonfiction book, *Between the World and Me.*

Critical Race Theory, Ibram X. Kendi and his Book How to be an Antiracist

A brutal, factual, logical dissection of Ibram X. Kendi's *How to be an Antiracist.*

Flawed from the Beginning

An Open Letter to Ibram X Kendi About His Book, Stamped from the Beginning

Mr. Kendi's award winning, revisionist American history is driven by his anti-racist political agenda, making it rotten with errors, omissions and falsifications. Flawed from the Beginning exposes Mr. Kendi's butchery of our shared American story.

Eight Days in October

While searching for his missing father, sixteen-year-old Simon Cubbins unravels a decades old mystery that brings him into violent conflict with ghouls, ghosts, murderers and – worst of all – his own estranged family. Adult readers only.

Summer of the Toad

A rollicking woodland adventure featuring Toadley Smith, an amphibian on a mission to rescue his mouse lab assistant from ravenous gang of four-fingered raccoons. For all ages.

Hamlet in Modern Verse

A faithful rendering of The Bard's classic tragedy for modern readers. Written in rhyme.

Trailer Park Classics Presents: Romeo and Juliette

A comedic reimagining of Romeo and Juliette set in a modern day trailer park. Written in rhyme.

When Sharkadillos Attack!!!

An eclectic, chaotic assortment of anecdotes, fake news articles, diary entries, movie reviews and more that are as sure to offend as they are to amuse. Adult readers only.

PREFACE

Even though *The Cult of Critical Theory* was written as a reaction to the ubiquitous negativity permeating American society today, it is a pro-humanity and pro-unity book. This writing supports truth and rejects intentional falsifications.

The *Cult of Critical Theory* is not an attack on our university system of higher education as a whole. I've spent many beneficial years in this system, during which time I met scholars, researchers and professors whose intellectual honesty was unimpeachable.

This book very specifically exposes what we will soon discuss as 'Critical Theory,' those university-based intellectuals who spawned it and the activists, journalists and politicians who employ it to bitter ends.

I give sociologists specific and significant discredit, but I hope to prove that they've earned it. If my contempt for them is too apparent, I apologize in advance. My career as a physician has involved giving people hard and accurate truths about their pending miscarriage, their cancer diagnosis or new brain metastases, their heart attack, their spouse's death. I have little patience or empathy for academic pseudo-intellectuals whose careers involve fabricating false truths from their imaginations or their skewed views of society.

If this book is 'against' anything, it is against liars and bullies. I hope it reads as such.

I also hope everyone reading this book longs for social justice (an admittedly imprecise but valuable idea) and despises biased behavior and racist beliefs. And I hope everyone reading this book genuinely wants to promote an increasingly unified American identity that recognizes every individual's inherent worth and equally shared humanity. If my existence as a straight, White, educated, professional, abled male with a belief in the biologic underpinnings of sex (and the coexisting freedom to express unique gender identity) reflexively irritates you, then you might want to find another book.

Within we explore the false assumptions underlying such things as Critical Race Theory, Systemic Racism and White Supremacy. If you reflexively call such an effort 'racist' or charge that it reinforces 'White Supremacy,' you might want to find another book (while reassessing your ability to consider ideas that are unlike your own).

This book is about debunking false narratives. As the author, I want every Reader to know I recognize that American society has real and long-term problems with race, gender and gender identity. People in this country are being marginalized simply because of how they were born. This is wrong and un-American. A final, perfect, unified, ideal America is a worthy goal that we should all strive for even as we understand it can never be fully and finally reached. It is a process of progress that cannot and should not end.

If you chose to read on, you will be challenged to consider several uncomfortable but largely unassailable facts (and my many overt opinions) that counter the prevailing falsehoods. Falsehoods repeated so often they have become an alternate truth. Falsehoods fobbed off upon us by mistaken activists, misleading scholars and misinforming journalists and misguided politicians.

My sincere hope is that you read skeptically and critically. Maintain healthy doubt and check my facts and references. Then decide for yourself what *you* believe, even if you eventually dispute and reject everything that follows.

Countering false narratives about sensitive issues such as race and gender identity does not equate to an attack on either race or gender identity. Delving into the facts of painful cases like that of Breonna Taylor in no way diminishes Ms. Taylor's complex and inherently valuable humanity. Highlighting the lies of those who have commandeered the Black Lives Matter movement does lessen the inherent nobility and worth of Black lives.

Throughout this book, different racial groups are referred to as White, Black, Latino, Asian, Middle Eastern, Pacific Islander and Native American. None of these terms are meant to convey any offense. I recognize that, while as useful generalizations, they do not capture the vast differences within these groups.

CONSIDER...

"The media's the most powerful entity on earth. They have the power to make the innocent guilty and to make the guilty innocent."
- Malcolm X

"Whenever you find yourself on the side of the majority, it is time to pause and reflect."
- Mark Twain

"A true and worthy ideal frees and uplifts a people; a false ideal imprisons and lowers."
- W. E. B. Du Bois.

"In recognizing the humanity of our fellow beings, we pay ourselves the highest tribute."
-Thurgood Marshall.

"I am a firm believer in the people. If given the truth, they can be depended upon to meet any national crisis. The great point is to bring them the real facts."
- Abraham Lincoln

CHAPTER ONE.
WHAT CRITICAL THEORY IS AND ISN'T.

EUGENICS.

First, consider eugenics. Literally 'good genetics.' The outdated and disproven idea that certain groups of people have superior genetics while lower, 'mongrel' races are seeded with inferior DNA.

Near the beginning of the 20th century, this idea was grasped by a handful of intellectuals and turned into a 'science.' These were graduates from and professors at prestigious universities such as Columbia, Yale, Eton, King's College, Cornell and Stanford.

These academic elites churned out papers and books and the idea of eugenics gained traction. Eugenics became a legitimate field of study in the Sociology Departments of universities across America. Undergraduate courses in this subject flourished.

Proponents of eugenics widely believed in the superior 'inborn value' of the Nordic race over those inferior races from southern and western Europe and the Mediterranean. They feared that their preferred genetic stock would become diluted by a flood of 'beaten races' into the United States.

Professor Edward A. Ross coined the term 'race suicide' and wrote things like, "the race which excels in energy, self-reliance and education will have the advantage." (1).

Mr. Ross served as the fifth President of the American Sociological Society for the years 1914 and 1915 and helped create the American Association of University Professors. In 1929, Ross formed a separate Department of Sociology and Anthropology at the University of Wisconsin, which he chaired until his retirement in 1937. During his tenure, Ross wrote twenty-seven books and over three hundred articles. (2)

One of the most influential books on eugenics, *The Passing of the Great Race*, was written by Madison Grant and published in 1916. *Science* magazine reviewed the book in 1918 and concluded that Mr. Grant's "recent success is sufficiently justified, since he has written both boldly and attractively, and has produced a work of solid merit." It continued, "The present reviewer accepts, in the main, this racial theory of European historical anthropology" that is "supported by the facts of history." (3)

"Supported by the facts of history." This is important to remember because we will see many examples of historical facts being distorted and falsified for political activism as we proceed. This was the same *Science* magazine that is still published today by its original supporter, the American Association for the Advancement of Science.

The scientific 'fact' of eugenics was accepted in general society and influenced our politics. US immigration laws were changed and the barbaric practice of forced sterilization of so-called inferiors began. Overseas, Adolf Hitler read Grant's book while in prison writing *Mein Kampf*. As Führer, Hitler wrote to Grant to thank him and Hitler referred to Grant's book as his "Bible." (4)

Roughly one hundred years later, we recognize eugenics as a fatally flawed pseudo-science that caused immeasurable harm. But its brief and malignant life did demonstrate something very valuable. That is, a simple false idea can be claimed by academia, turned into belief and then into scientific fact.

Our self-appointed intellectual elites - sociologists and social scientists - did this. Eugenic 'facts' influenced public opinion and official State policy. Entire groups of people were stigmatized, marginalized and even villainized because of how they were born. Countless lives were adversely and permanently affected or even ended.

CLASSIC LIBERAL THOUGHT.

Have we learned from this?

Apparently not. The very same thing is happening today.

As with eugenics, our great universities have now taken the idea of Systemic Racism and turned it into a scientific fact. Career academics churn out books and articles to convince first themselves and then the general populace. All White people are, because they were born White, complicit in an invisible and omnipresent hierarchy of dominance and submission.

To understand how this occurred, we have to examine the roots and meanings of current Social

Justice and Identity Politics. We must understand the prevailing schools of thought in today's universities.

Classic 'liberal' thought prevailed from before America's inception into the 1960's and early 1970's. It still prevails outside of snarky social media forums and the scholarly pursuits of intellectuals insulated from the messy realities of the lives they mentally dissect from a safe distance. Liberal thought values an empowered individual, free expression and open, honest debate. Liberal ideals support religious freedom but not superstition or magical thinking. Liberal methods reinforce scientific, theoretical and philosophic reason that can sustain rigorous and repeated tests of their validity.

In short, liberal thought produced the types of ideas and exchanges you might hope to share with your physician or your dinner companion. Conversations that might negate some of your ideas and beliefs (or reinforce them) while leaving you more informed, aware and enlightened. Liberal thinkers, scholars, scientists and activists propelled America's greatest economic, political, technologic and social progress.

Liberal thought in its essential form is a sort of ceaseless, restless natural selection of ideas. It constantly challenges what is known and what is accepted and retains only that which is valid and humane while discarding what is false and cruel. It is an imperfect, uneven and stuttering path toward an unreachable perfect state of knowing and being.

So long as an individual remains curious and open minded, they likely employ liberal thought mechanics constantly and often unconsciously. Those rooted in ignorance, cognitive apathy, prejudice and hate have likely forsaken liberal thought and settled into a quagmire of stubborn bias.

Note that this classic definition of 'liberal' thought does not link it to or separate it from any current American political party. Ideally, all of our elected representatives – Republican, Democrat and Independent - would employ liberal thinking, though much sad evidence suggests otherwise. Both political extremes can claim liberal thought even as they twist it to malignant ends. Far Right populists and White Nationalists can pervert truth and reason as vigorously and effectively as those on the extreme Left.

Early17th century liberal thinkers challenged and opposed the false racial dogma of slave traders and slave owners. These Abolitionists, as they came to be called, valued the universal humanity of every individual and rejected the assumption that some peoples were inherently inferior. This focus on universal humanity is in direct opposition to Identity Politics, which tends to divide and sub-divide humanity. These Abolitionists were perhaps the first Social Justice advocates in North America, even when this 'America' was still entirely British in culture, citizenship, attitude, law and practice.

Liberal thought inherently opposes blind prejudice, unthinking political orthodoxy, hateful theocracy and fascist regimes of any type. All of mankind's history is the record of our hard-won successes and tragic failures. Point to any of our darkest moments in the age of liberal thought – the American slave trade, the Brazilian slave trade, the Barbary Coast pirates who enslaved White Europeans, the enslavement of Slavs and Jews by the Nazis,

Japan's forced labor camps and systematic mass rapes of conquered women during WW II, the ongoing forced conscription of Africa's child soldiers, the present coercive flow unwilling sex workers – and you can find examples of liberal-minded individuals and groups of all races fighting to disrupt them.

THE RISE OF POSTMODERNISM.

Classic liberal thought faced serious doubt from prominent philosophers following two World Wars, the second of which overtly harnessed scientific breakthroughs to create mass crematoriums, faster planes that could deliver heavier destructive payloads, deadlier tanks, radar detection devices and the atomic bomb. World War Two was also preceded by Hitler's perversion of the philosophies of intellectual giants such Sigmund Freud and Friedrich Nietzsche in order to justify his extermination camps, bloody purges and crushing subjugation of 'inferior,' non-Teutonic peoples – the Czechs, the Poles, the Russians, etc.

These thinkers also saw the rise of post-war prosperity with its accompanying conformity and materialism. They witnessed the signing of the Warsaw Pact and rebuilding of the Soviet Union with all of its inhumanity and violence and oppression. This was a new atomic age in which a mad man in a bunker could obliterate populations or entire nations with the push of a button. The British Colonial Empire crumbled, and millions died in India alone during its turbulent birth as an independent nation and its violent separation from its previously conjoined sibling, Pakistan.

The philosophy generated from these intellectuals coalesced into a nihilistic negation of liberal thought. This became Postmodernism. Postmodernist philosophers looked at a shattered and chaotic world confronted by the ever-present existential threat of nuclear annihilation. At the same time, this world was increasingly consumerist, complacent and superficially comfortable (for most, but not all).

While there is no definite timeline, many suggest the Postmodernist movement occurred in the second half of the 20th century. This was from the early 1940's, when Hitler's boot smothered most of Europe, to the early 1990's, when panic over the AIDs crisis began to fade, the Soviet Union imploded and bands like Nirvana and Soundgarden were vanquishing vapid 1980's pop music.

Liberal thought and its adherence to sound reason, reproducible scientific methods and objective truth had seemingly failed. The Postmodernists conducted their autopsy and found liberal methods fundamentally flawed, because mankind could never realize any final, fundamental, universal 'Truth.'

Since liberal thought could apparently not propel humanity ever-closer toward an ultimate Truth, the Postmodernists believed mankind was doomed to forever orbit around theoretical Truths. During these futile cycles, mankind would dwell within artificial, corrupt, social 'truth frameworks.' These social frameworks were created by those atop any socio-political hierarchy and maintained via regulation of what people say and how they are able to say it (their available means of 'discourse').

Knowledge, reason, morality, religion and science were myths created in any given society in order to maintain the existing power structure. Those embedded within these social frameworks were unaware of it and unknowingly aided and abetted their overlords by holding discourse in the means deemed socially proper. All knowledge was unique to that system and all beliefs were inherently political.

Importantly, the Postmodernists felt no single framework was preferable or morally superior to any other. Morals were simply social and political constructs of oppression. The Postmodernists felt there was no objective way to measure one framework against any other. No society could rightly claim more truth or morality, because all societies were built on artificial and transient truths.

These Postmodernists were largely content to stew in their own bleak pessimism. Their fanciful yet dreary thought exercises had little pragmatic or 'actionable' value. They were mainly thinkers and philosophers, not activists. But they added greatly to and changed the trajectory of the interwoven concept of 'Critical Theory' (or simply 'Theory').

Critical Theory is a social philosophy that investigates society and culture in order to understand their inherent power structures. Theory's originators in 1930's Germany intended it to be activist in nature. Critical Theorists intended not just to simply observe society, but to actively manipulate it.

More recent Critical Theory holds that any given society's ills (poverty, racism, sexism, etc.) are caused by the oppressive hierarchical power dynamics inherent in that society. That unique society's morals, history, knowledge, cultural assumptions, laws, superstitions and even its common courtesies and grammar exist in a social framework of dominance and oppression. This framework is maintained in overt ways (court decisions, educational practices, religious teachings, etc.) and in unconscious ways via reinforcing expected social norms.

The Postmodernists intense focus on the power of language and discourse as the means to maintain socio-political power dynamics was arguably their main influence on subsequent Critical Theory. The words we use and how we say them achieve binary ends – they either maintain or disrupt power systems. And these power systems are inherently corrupt simply because they are inherently oppressive.

THE AGE OF THE APPLIED POSTMODERN THEORIST.

Enter the age of the Applied Postmodern Theorists. These were scholar-activists who sought not to just deconstruct society in the passive, depressing Postmodern fashion. They meant to actively reconstruct society in their vision of Social Justice. Applied Postmodern Theorists took the nebulous nihilism of the Postmodern thinkers and imbued it with their purposeful, self-righteous, self-important activist nihilism. Applied Postmodern Theory adherents remained a very pessimistic bunch.

These individuals formed part of what we'll call the intelligentsia. Their work solely entails ideas and abstractions. The intelligentsia manipulates concepts that elude rigid standards of reproducible science. Theories that rely on peer consensus for validity. Philosophers and sociologists create such generalizations and inferences and then agree among themselves which to promote as true. Sometimes they encourage concepts that propel society's enlightenment. Sometimes, as with eugenics, they unleash hell.

A messy and contradictory marriage between seething Social Justice and slippery Identity Politics was then ordained by their new religion – Critical Theory. This school of thought demands that every facet of a given society exists only to perpetuate the current power structure. This includes the simplest mundane acts such as asking for directions to the most abstract concepts such as the elusive nature of thought, time, space, knowledge and, literally, all aspects of reality.

As with eugenics, these ideas first took root in universities. Scholarly intellectuals latched on to the idea of oppressive hierarchies and accepted it as fact. With such a wild new sandbox to play in, the intelligentsia sifted through, rearranged and reshaped human history and scientific knowledge. Then they reduced American society in all of its varying layers of intricate complexity down to the single, simple, self-serving social framework of dominance and oppression.

With this reductionist assumption in place, our trusted university scholars began spewing research articles that merely cited other scholars in order to create new theories, paradigms and 'ways of knowing.' All of this was codified in vast swamps of intellectual jargon not unlike the phrases invented to give eugenics a scientific sheen. Once these intellectuals had accumulated a proper critical mass of new facts, all prior understanding was discredited or discarded.

As Critical Theory took root, it sprouted many sickly branches. Critical Race Theory. Critical Gender Theory. Critical Feminist Theory. Critical Queer Theory. Each Theory views modern society through the lens of the presumably oppressed group.

CRITICAL RACE THEORY.

Thus, American Critical Race Theory views all the myriad facets of our modern society through the single lens of race. Critical Race Theory assumes that the majority group – whites – unknowingly serve their racist overlords simply by participating in society, a society built around invisible, self-sustaining, oppressive racial hierarchies. This 'Systemic Racism' affords the majority 'White Privilege' and 'White Supremacy.' When white people are informed of their constant, unconscious, racist actions, they demonstrate their 'White Fragility' by protesting. This denial only serves to prove their racist white guilt. As Ibram X Kendi wrote on page 14 of *How to be an Antiracist*, "Denial is the heartbeat of racism"

Summarizing Critical Race Theory on page 15 of his book, Mr. Kendi stated that one "either believes problems are rooted in groups of people, as a racist, or locates the roots of problems in power and policies, as an antiracist." Which policies? Mr. Kendi outlines this on page 29. These include "written and unwritten laws, rules procedures, processes, regulations, and guidelines that govern people." And on page 30, "Racism itself is institutional, structural, and systemic."

Robin Diangelo reinforces Critical Race Theory's broad assumptions in her book White Fragility." On page 72, Ms. Diangelo wrote, "Racism is a systemic, societal, institutional, omnipresent and epistemologically embedded phenomenon the pervades every vestige of our reality." She wrote on the same page, "If we cannot discuss these dynamics or see ourselves within them, we cannot stop participating in racism."

This is Critical Race Theory. It is the assumption that highly charged racial issues permeate all of our official and unofficial institutions and all written and unwritten rules governing behavior down to the smallest trace of existence. It exists in conveniently vague 'structures' and 'policies' that White people are guilty of propagating and supporting just by living within this presumed racial hierarchy.

With Critical Race Theory, every action or inaction that adversely affects a person of color is a racist action, even if that action was performed by another person of color. As Ta-Nehisi Coates pointed out in *Between the World and Me*, page 17, "To be black in the Baltimore of my youth was to be naked before the elements of the world, before all the guns, fists, knives, crack, rape, and disease. The nakedness is not an error, nor pathology. The nakedness is the correct and intended result of policy, the predictable upshot of people forced for centuries to live under fear. The law did not protect us." Mr. Coates added "These new [white] people are, like us [black people], a modern invention. But unlike us, their new name has no real meaning divorced from the machinery of criminal power."

The machinery of criminal power that is rooted in policies and affects every vestige of our reality. Wow.

Critical Theory and its many offshoots are inherently agenda-driven. They seek to promote their warped version of Social Justice by toppling oppressive hierarchies. Social and political agendas are anathema to pure scholarship, untainted research and reproducible scientific facts. Thus, no matter how strenuously these Critical Theory intellectuals and activists try to show the purely academic, peer-reviewed, scientifically-constructed and 'factually-based' nature of their oppressive hierarchies, they can never be separated from their political agenda. Their 'research' is faulty at its inception.

Hard sciences such as molecular biology (which yields helpful actualities like the polymerase chain reaction) and physics (with its predictable and reproducible vectors of motion) contribute concretely and often permanently to mankind's base of knowledge. Sociology, a soft science, might offer insight into fundamental truisms of society and theories of how and why societies change. But, as with eugenics, their theories can mutate into something dangerous.

Robin Diangelo's *New York Times* bestselling book *White Fragility* exemplifies how Postmodern Critical Theory can infest a scholar's misunderstanding of the world. On the first page of the forward Ms. Diangelo allows this to be stated: "[Whiteness is] at once a means of dominance, the means to which dominance points and the point of dominance, too, which, in its purest form, in its greatest fantasy, never ends" and Whiteness "in the jargon of the academy is termed social construct, an agreed upon myth that has empirical grit because of its effect, not its essence." This myopic view of the world, viewed through the single, sordid lens of Critical Race Theory, has become a cognitive epidemic.

The pseudo-scholarly support of Critical Race Theory attracted politicians and journalists. With the newly minted, 'evidence-based facts' of Systemic Racism and White Supremacy in hand, a vast new lexicon of ideas blossomed like bitter little flowers. The ideas spread and White Supremacy became belief. Belief coalesced into orthodoxy. Preaching the orthodoxy of Critical Race Theory became virtue while any doubt became racist blaspheme. Whiteness became a social disease that traumatized marginalized groups. Social Justice was the savior and White Supremacy was Satan.

On page two of the forward to *White Fragility*, Ms. Robin Diangelo actually allowed an overt comparison between Whiteness and the "Devil." It's in print. Page three of the forward stated that "straight white men" are the "nemeses" to democracy, truth and justice. Again, this is the forward. We're not even into the Author's Note or the subsequent Introduction, let alone the main text.

In the children's book, *Not My Idea: A Book About Whiteness*, one illustration depicts a devil holding a "contract binding you to whiteness." The contract offers "stolen land, stolen riches" and "to mess endlessly with...all fellow humans of color." The opposite page informs young children that, "Whiteness is a bad deal. It always was." This book is being used in kindergarten classes in Evanston, IL. (5)

21

An Article for *The Root* titled *Whiteness is a Pandemic* states "Whiteness is a public health crisis. It shortens life expectancies, it pollutes air, it constricts equilibrium, it devastates forests, it melts ice caps, it sparks (and funds) wars, it flattens dialects, it infests consciousnesses, and it kills people," and the author added "White supremacy is a virus that, like other viruses, will not die until there are no bodies left for it to infect. Which means the only way to stop it is to locate it, isolate it, extract it, and kill it." (6) *The Root* is an online magazine owned by Univision Communications, which had a revenue of $2.7 billion in 2018.

An article for *Psychology Today* stated "What is Whiteness? An unfairly privileged exclusionary category, based on physical features, most notably a lack of melanin," and "one should not be proud of one's Whiteness. Whiteness is a forced group membership that originated by oppressing people of color" while "pride in Blackness represents pride in the accomplishments and resilience of a racialized group in the face of continual oppression." It concluded, "It is hoped that those who are able to see the tragedy of Whiteness will reject it." (7)

Whiteness is the Devil. Whiteness must be killed. The tragedy of Whiteness. Again, we're discussing a very pessimistic bunch of people. Sadly, these same people perhaps genuinely yearn for progress in racial equality, gender equality and gender-identity equality. I'll suggest that by portraying the majority of US citizens as a homogenous, tragic, demonic force that needs to be killed, these writers subvert their own cause.

There is no doubt that White Supremacists exist. They are usually not shy about spouting their own caustic, degrading and so-called 'scientific' beliefs. And there is no doubt that significant racial prejudice and its pernicious effects still linger in America. But this author rejects any philosophy founded on hate and whose outcome, if not inherent purpose, is to increase social division and anger. I reject any orthodoxy whose adherents perpetuate blatant falsehoods and cruel intolerance. I take such things as personal insults.

Consider the parallels between eugenics and current Critical Race Theory. It's impressive that such sad, sloppy, pseudo-scientific social philosophies can be dressed up in academic jargon and pawned off by intellectuals as factual and even logical.

IDENTITY POLITICS.

These Theory-minded sociologists now splinter marginalized groups into ever increasing numbers, compounding their many 'intersections of trauma.' If you exist as a person of color, a woman, a homosexual, a transgendered person or a person with a disability, then you suffer social trauma even if you did not know it. If a sociologist can assign you several identity tags, you then suffer multiple social traumas at every intersection of these existences. Straight White males, by this definition, can only inflict social trauma, they cannot suffer from it.

This idea of 'intersecting traumas' came from a group of Black, feminist, lesbian, Marxist-Socialists in 1977. These women had a three-year series of

23

meetings and finally published *The Combahee River Collective*. They advocated the "destruction of the political-economic systems of capitalism." They hoped their White feminist counterparts could "have a more than superficial comprehension" of Black culture and stated that "even our Black women's style of talking / testifying in Black language" had profound cultural and political effects.

This division into disparate identity groups is in stark contrast to the ideas of classic liberal activists. Martin Luther King Junior and Malcolm X, despite their differences, both preached of the shared human dignity of all colors and sought to bring them into greater harmony. They sought to reduce prejudice by underscoring the inherent, common humanity that unites all people. They argued that this shared normative state entitled everyone to equal rights and expressive freedoms. They believed in a universal truth that all could and should strive toward together. And they had great success.

Identity Politics is the antithesis of this liberal idea. In Identity Politics, any "normative" is oppressive. The adherents to Identity Politics divide people and reduce the individual's identity into charged political categories, whichever categories are most useful to their current crusade. Scholars and activists then aggressively and almost obsessively scour discourse for ways in which marginalized groups might suffer offense, any offense, offenses wrenched from benign speech and unintentional inferences or even potential offenses not yet committed.

Identity Politics assumes and reinforces differences, not commonalities. This unintentionally belittles the marginalized groups in paternalistic ways, constantly reinforcing their status as oppressed victims. All this while divisively alienating 'oppressor' groups with ceaseless charges of racism, sexism, ableism, homophobia, transphobia and so forth. Instead of marching together, unified, toward a shared common purpose, we remain forever divided, forever oppressed and / or forever guilty.

Perhaps this is what it now means to be 'woke' in American society. Being woke means accepting the pessimistic, false narrative of Theory and then seeing intersecting traumas everywhere, all the time, in every interaction with Whiteness. Being woke means seeing all of this and believing it without question. Being woke means accepting all of this on faith. Being woke means reflexively reinforcing this orthodoxy without the burdensome process of independent critical thinking.

CURRENT EXAMPLES IN ACTION.

Take the case of Mr. Emmanuel Cannady. Mr. Cannady is a member of the Black Lives Matter Global Network's South Bend chapter. He cast himself upon the national stage when he appeared in a BLM video on June 2nd 2020. As of March 2021, he was also a PhD candidate in sociology at Notre Dame.

Delving deeply, if not articulating, into the jargon of Identity Politics and demonstrating his faith in Critical Race Theory orthodoxy, Mr. Cannady said (38:19) "Yeah, something that we've, um, been in the works on is starting, um, a part of our organization called Black Queer Lives Matter in realizing that, uh, people experience intersecting traumas in intersecting experiences of, of domination through, at, at different levels." (8)

As of March 15, 2021, Mr. Cannady's homepage (on sociology.nd.eud) included "Emmanuel's research deals broadly with race and ethnicity, trauma, racialization, family, social movements, and the sociology of knowledge. His main research agenda interrogates the racialized meanings of interpersonal interactions across different contexts, including social movement organizations, bystander intervention, friendships, and partner selection to reveal the complex reality of race in the 21st century. For his dissertation, Emmanuel participates in a chapter of the Black Lives Matter Global Network to investigate how intersecting levels of trauma affect activists' creation and deployment of different types of knowledge."

This single paragraph encapsulates everything wrong with the university system today (or at least its humanities departments). Mr. Cannady's entire, expensive education is based on elusive and illusory Critical Race Theory power hierarchies, a single school of thought that short-sighted or bored or unimaginative or cunning intellectuals allowed to consume all other schools of thought in their own minds.

Instead of a world wherein mankind is liberated by free discourse and experimentation and an ever-growing, virile body of shared knowledge, they foist upon us this corpulent, diseased Theory. A Theory that reads racialization and trauma into all human interactions. A Theory telling us that knowledge itself is a smothering plague inflicted by

Whiteness upon minority groups to stifle their myriad 'other knowledges.' It is a sickly pseudo-science that defies common definition and can only be 'researched' by generating and rearranging new, equally undefinable and unprovable ideas and then dressing them up in the increasingly pretentious, impenetrable and ultimately meaningless jargon of academia.

This is not any indictment of Mr. Cannady himself. He is a product of his time and a victim of his mentors. It is sad to see his PhD level intellect channeled into such conjectural whimsies as "the sociology of knowledge." It is disheartening to see him and the woke sheep like him assume that such vague metaphysical concepts can somehow be 'researched' via the same scientific methods that the disciples of Applied Postmodern Critical Theory negate as oppressive.

Consider Professor Frank Leon Roberts, a faculty member at New York University's Gallatin School of Individualized Study. Mr. Roberts created the course "Black Lives Matter: Race, Resistance, and Populist Protest" (9) which examines the traumatic 'intersections' of race and gender in America.

In a March 4, 2021, online classroom discussion, guest speaker Deray McKesson stated (9:42) "So the logic of policing says there are people with power who makes rules and they enforce those rules on people without power."

Professor Roberts responded (10:27), "I love that. So, in other words, that, as you say here, law enforcement is simply a reflection of a broader system of policing that has certain structural qualities, which

principle of humanity does not make the prevailing group inherently and maliciously 'oppressive.'

For a society to function, there has to be a 'normative' standard. If every permutation of human behavior becomes normative, then pedophilia and necrophilia cease to be abnormal. In this case we sink into a murky soup of moral relativism where presumptions of privacy, autonomy and personal property become ambiguous to the point of vanishing. Conversely, if nothing can be normative (if everything is considered aberrant), then society either devolves into chaos or into an absolute police state of homogenous stasis and constant mutual suspicion.

Social norms are necessary but are not necessarily static. They change over time (and not always for the better). Such norms allow us to establish a working cognitive construct of the world around us. Liberal thought then allows us to challenge these norms, to expand upon them, to affirm them and to revise them.

Such norms are inherently flexible and always changing. Take any identifiable social group you can think of. What was this group's station and beliefs in society one hundred years ago? What is it today? How does that group's current station and beliefs in American society compare to similar people in the Central African Republic? In Venezuela? In Afghanistan? In China?

Critical Theory, in stark contrast, locks us into rigid oppressive hierarchies. Whiteness founded America as a racist nation and Whiteness has never and can never change. This is, again, an absurdly reductionist assertion.

Theory-minded sociologists say that White people have been 'socialized' to hold preconceptions of all people of color. This occurs via "television, movies, news items, stories, jokes, traditions and practices, history, and so on." (10)

I accept this as generally true.

But these sociologists then go on to apparently make several grandiose and flawed assumptions that they fob off as truth. Every White person's socialized preconceptions are inherently negative (apparently television, movies, religion and so on have somehow never portrayed any positive images of People of Color). These inherently negative preconceptions are identical in every White person, everywhere in America. These inherently negative, identical, White preconceptions are unchanging through time (through an individual's lifetime and across generations). And finally, White people lack the insight and 'racial stamina' to acknowledge, analyze, understand, challenge and change their inherently negative, identical, unchanging preconceptions.

I reject all of these as blatantly false.

The very ideas of Systemic Racism and White Supremacy are not only gross oversimplifications of an infinitely complex nation (and remember, they are just ideas). They also ignore or negate the millions of Blacks, Latinos, Asians, Middle Eastern, Pacific Islander and Native Americans of both sexes and all gender identities who have profoundly and permanently influenced (or 'socialized') American culture and our shared 'systems' (governance, education, law, etc.).

These collective People of Color have included coaches, Supreme Court Justices, Attorneys General, college professors, physicians, inventors, investors, surgeons, scientists, Secretaries of State, athletes, actors, activists, authors, pastors, police and a US President. The author of *White Fragility* curtly dismisses such people and their societal contributions. On page 27 she actually wrote that these influential People of Color "support the status quo and do not challenge racism in any way significant enough to be threatening." Her example here included Barack Obama and Clarence Thomas.

Theory-minded sociologists cannot dissect out this long running, cumulative, massive contribution away from 'White America.' Activists ignore the intricate threads of Color sewn into every inch of our collective consciousness. But no one can negate the still-rippling effects of people like Harriet Tubman, Cesar Chavez, Condoleezza Rice, Bruce Lee, Maya Angelou, Eric Holder and Miles Davis on all Americans.

Briefly consider the attempts by American 'Whiteness' to diminish itself. It is well beyond the scope of this writing to outline everything from the 1688 Germantown Quaker Petition Against Slavery to the election of Vice President Kamala Harris. But this long and turbulent but fruitful process has made America arguably the greatest country on earth to be a Person of Color, a woman and / or one with a non-traditional gender identity. People of all Colors, including Whites, have aided this process. Sociologists and other adherents to Theory, in my studies, have made no credible attempt to explain these issues away.

Essentially, the Cult of Critical Theory states that White culture is internally and unconsciously flawed and remains forever unaffected by the 'external' influence of People of Color. Conversely, Theory seems to imply the cultures of People of Color are internally flawless and any problems within them are caused exclusively by the pernicious external force of Whiteness.

Of course, no culture exists at any discreet point of pristine perfection or total toxicity. But when the devotees of Critical Theory begin to recognize nuances, contradictions and varying degrees of exceptions to their rigid rules (that is, facts and practical realities that counter ideology), their lofty, self-righteous tower begins to crack and tremble.

Scholarly intellectuals also persist with the notion that North American Whiteness is somehow unique in history because of colonialism and the subjugation and enslavement of other people. But any honest historian or anthropologist easily can refute this.

Consider the Ming Dynasty's centuries-long use of slaves to build the 13,000-mile-long Great Wall. The ancient Pharos' use of slaves to erect the Great Pyramids. The slaves in India who built the Taj Mahal. The captured Jews who provided unskilled labor to erect the Roman Coliseum. The Precolonial Native American tribes that used slave labor. If the women of the conquering Indian tribe so demanded, these captives could be ritually tortured, sometimes to death, if the captive was deemed unfit. (11)

White convicts were sent to Australia and forced into slave labor as punishment for their crimes. They toiled alongside the Aborigines and Pacific

Islanders who were forced into servitude there. Genghis Khan was a Mongol invader who sexually enslaved conquered women. His whose quests for more land were often accompanied by large-scale massacres of the civilian populations. Captives and other conquered people served as slaves for Khan's extended family. Slavery persists across the African continent to this day.

These are only a few of the examples of any given culture's tireless and often brutal quest to secure resources for and expand the influence of its own people. None of these examples can ever excuse America's own barbaric use of slave labor. But it is a false narrative to single out 'Whiteness' (that universally damning, dehumanizing, blanket term covering billions of people) as the sole perpetrator of slavery. Slaying such false narratives in the name of truth is the aim of this book.

ASAIN AMERICANS AND CRITICAL RACE THEORY.

Theory-minded sociologists and Social Justice activists avoid mentioning the most successful People of Color. Asian Americans typically outpace all other racial group – including Whites – in every measurable category: literacy, loan approval rates, household income, (lower) incarceration rates, high school graduation rates, longevity, GPA's and standardized test scores, attainment of bachelor's degrees, employment permanence (Whites are fired or furloughed before Asian Americans), credit scores, and as directors of global box office champion movies.

Sociologists rooted in Critical Theory and current activists are vexed by the stubborn upward trajectory and annoying achievements of people of Asian descent. Asian Americans undermine Critical RaceTheory's sickly presumptions and are thus discreetly ignored. Including such information would devastate Critical Theory. The intelligentsia highlight only that statistical data that reinforces their ideas of discrimination in America. They intentionally ignore any data that counters their narrative.

There is research that helps explain the disparities between Asian Americans and their White peers. Some researchers have produced evidence that cultural differences between Asian American families and White American families mitigate any Socio-economic effects on Asian American children's academic achievement. That is, even poor Asian American children tend to outperform their wealthier White peers.

One study, for example, found that "Asian Americans' behaviors and attitudes are less influenced by family SES [socio-economic status] than those of Whites are and that this difference helps generate Asians' premium in achievement. This is especially evident at lower levels of family SES." (12) Otherwise stated, the poorer the White family, the worse their kids do academically. Asian Americans' academic success is much less affected by poverty.

Another study found that Asian-Americans' educational advantage is largely due to these students exerting greater academic effort "and not to advantages in tested cognitive abilities or socio-demographics." (13) This study also found that, compared to White households, the parents of Asian

American students tend to be both better educated and married. However, even relatively disadvantaged children of Chinese and Vietnamese immigrant families routinely surpassed the academic success of their middle-class white peers.

This study offers evidence that academic success is determined by both cognitive ability and a multidimensional set of capabilities referred to as 'noncognitive skills.' These skills include, self-control, attentiveness, motivation and persistence and that these skills "may be as important as cognitive abilities in positively affecting academic performance."

How do Asian American students learn such skills? This study states that Asian-American parents not only have higher educational expectations but are also "more authoritarian and less permissive than white American families." (13)

Based on these studies, it appears that Asian American families tend to have a stronger nucleus and maintain a culture that promotes discipline and perseverance. These cultural advantages persist even in poorer Asian American households. **These findings demonstrate that culture, not race or household income, can raise People of Color upward in our shared social hierarchies. This concept is the antithesis (the anti-theory) of Critical Race Theory.**

PRACTICAL EXAMPLES THAT UNDERMINE CRITICAL RACE THEORY.

Critical Race Theory claims that any disparity between any majority Group A and any minority

Group B is inherently egregious, if not immoral. Any disparity is because Group A asserts some nefarious, hierarchal, external pressure down upon Group B. Group A's achievement becomes 'privilege' wrought by the deprivation of Group B. Critical Race Theory stops there.

I fully acknowledge that there are many examples in America's long history where this has been true. Black Americans have long suffered the effects of the malignant afterbirth of slavery (Jim Crow laws, segregation, workplace discrimination, red lining, etc.).

But to stop there and ignore the effect of current internal culture is to ignore real opportunities for success. The intelligentsia cannot consider or even acknowledge this possibility. To be so evenhanded and look fairly at all variables would rob from them the 'Devil' of Whiteness and effectively end the Cult of Critical Theory.

Ms. Diangelo explicitly does just this on page 44 of *White Fragility*. She states that you demonstrate "Aversive Racism" if you attribute "inequality between whites and people of color to causes other than racism." In short, you are a racist if you think outside of the narrow confines of Critical Race Theory that call you racist.

But disparities between groups has been the rule in every society that has ever existed, not the exception. The reasons for this are as complex as the societies themselves. **Critical Race Theory does not consider (or even allow us to consider) the complex host other possible variables that explain disparities.**

Consider the lower median age of most People of Color. If a group's median age is lower, it likely has less collective education and work experience. This results in less accumulated wealth and fewer educational and professional accolades and accomplishments. If everything else was equal, *median age alone* would cause disparities.

Consider that compared to Whites and Asians, Black, Latino and Native American parents to be much younger on average when they begin having children. The real costs and the opportunity costs of raising children limit continuing education and workplace experience. Younger parents are generally less educated and less available for full time employment while also bearing the expense of raising children.

Critical Race Theory fails to consider geographic distribution and its effect on health. More than half of all Black people live in just those 16 States comprising the 'South.' *The Reasons for Geographic and Racial Differences in Stroke (REGARDS)* study (14) examined white and black adults aged 45 years and older from 2003 to 2007. This study identified the "Southern Dietary Pattern" that favored more sweets, more added fats and more fried foods. This diet was associated with a 56% higher risk of stroke. Many of these southern states also have the highest rates of obesity and cigarette consumption.

This heavier burden of illness could also explain disparities between groups. If you are more afflicted by chronic disease, you are less able to maintain employment.

Critical Race Theory doesn't consider the lower rates of households lead by married parents among

People of Color. Households lead by married parents are typically (but by no means universally) more financially stable are produce children better equipped to succeed in school.

Consider the power of language. Spoken and written language is the storehouse of a society's knowledge. The more fluent and literate you are in your language, the more knowledge you can access. A mastery of the English language in an English-speaking society is an obvious asset. First generation immigrants lacking English skills are naturally at a disadvantage in the workplace and the classroom. And, while there is value in the robust English dialects across America (Appalachian English, Black English, Pennsylvania Dutch English, etc.), they can become obstacles in arenas where 'standard' English is required. Those lacking standard English abilities will be disadvantaged in those arenas.

Moral abstractions aside, absorbing the maximum amount of knowledge and conveying the broadest range of ideas requires standard English skills in the United States. Anyone who argues otherwise has abandoned rational thought for agenda-based ideology.

Consider parallel disparities that do not involve race. Examine West Virginia. According to US census data:

In 2019, the median household income in the United States was $68,703 The median household income in West Virginia at that time was $46,711.

In 2019, the median value of owner-occupied housing units in West Virginia was $119,600 compared to a national average of $217,500.

In 2019, West Virginian households were less likely to own a computer or have internet access than the national average.

From 2016 to 2019 the poverty rate in West Virginia was 15.6%. Only two states were poorer. Louisiana was the poorest at 19.1% and New Mexico was at 17.2%. The national average poverty rate was 10.5%.

While students in West Virginia were more likely to complete high school than the national average, they were 31% less likely to get any graduate degree.

According to nationsreportcard.gov, the average 2019 mathematics score of fourth and fifth grade students in West Virginia was lower than the average score for public school students in the nation. In fact, 46 states scored higher than West Virginia and only Puerto Rico scored lower (three other states tied WV's score).

According to US census data, West Virginia was overwhelmingly White in 2019. The state had a Black population of 4.3% compared to a national average of 14.2% among all states. West Virginia also had a Latino population of only 1.3%.

Why do citizens in West Virginia, one of the Whitest states in the nation, suffer such obvious disparities if we exist in a system built on White Supremacy? Critical Theory has spawned Critical Race Theory and Critical Gender Theory (among others). Should we introduce a Critical Appalachian Theory? Is there some invisible framework of oppression keeping West Virginians poorer and less educated?

Of course not. Geography alone likely accounts for much of these disparities. West Virginia is largely rural, landlocked and mountainous. This makes travel difficult and regional isolation almost certain. Many remote pockets of the state suffer social stagnation.

Critical Theorists are wrong to assume that race is the *only* variable when looking at disparities affecting People of Color. This limited view intentionally excludes other variables that, if properly investigated, could yield opportunities for progress.

I'll share the Theorist's pessimism for a moment. Theorists obsessively look for problems. Actual solutions would rob them of any pretense to continue their sordid, sorry, pseudo-science.

Critical Race Theory is just a theory. Anyone could make the inverse theory and it would be equally valid (that is, not valid at all). Critical Anti-Theory might state that society exists as a framework of active producers above being drained by lower passive absorbers below. In this ridiculous framework, all means of discourse serve only to protect the absorber from having to become a producer. Such a theory should rightly be deemed offensive.

This Anti-Theory would have no more and no less pure merit than Critical Race Theory in the realm of ideas. These ideas have only the worth and moral weight that we give them. Today's social justice warriors reflexively cry 'racism' when Critical Race Theory is challenged by facts, counter-evidence and reason-based inquiries. Critical Race Theory therefor exists in a vacuum of liberal, intelligent thought. People used to call such vacuums ignorance. They would still be right today.

Regardless of its blatant contradictions, Theory is now everywhere. It's been repeated so often and so sincerely and the social consequences for doubting it are so real (ask JK Rowling), that it has become a meta-narrative, a framework of oppression. Theory has constricted our available means of discourse and set up a false hierarchy with the 'woke' on top and those who value factual evidence are unrestricted thought below. Unless you maintain healthy skepticism, you'll unknowingly perpetuate this perverse hierarchy of falsification over truth. So, check facts. Dive down those rabbit holes of reason. Think for yourself. Then decide what you believe.

THE EFFECTS OF CRITICAL THEORY.

Those purveyors of our current, misguided forms of Social Justice and Identity Politics must want some result. What have they produced?

A Pew Research poll in 2019 stated, "A majority of Americans say race relations in the United States are bad, and of those, about seven-in-ten say things are getting even worse." (15) The article attributed this to Donald Trump's Presidency, but a longitudinal Gallop poll suggests otherwise. From 2002 to 2012, 71% of White adults and 63% of Black adult respondents held a 'very good' or 'somewhat good' view of race relations. This dropped most sharply in 2013 and more gradually since to a low in 2020 of only 46% of Whites and 36% of Blacks saying the same. (16)

A July 2015 article in the *New York Times* stated, "nearly six in 10 Americans, including heavy majorities of both whites and blacks, think race relations are generally bad, and that nearly four in 10 think the situation is getting worse. By comparison, two-thirds of Americans surveyed shortly after President Obama took office said they believed that race relations were generally good." (17)

This article added, "During Mr. Obama's 2008 campaign, nearly 60 percent of blacks said race relations were generally bad, but that number was cut in half shortly after he won. It has now soared to 68 percent, the highest level of discontent among blacks during the Obama years and close to the numbers recorded in the aftermath of the riots that followed the 1992 acquittal of Los Angeles police officers charged in the beating of Rodney King." Again, that was in 2015.

Another 2015 poll showed that "Sixty-one percent of Americans now say race relations in this country are generally bad. That figure is up sharply from 44 percent after the fatal police shooting of Michael Brown and the unrest that followed in Ferguson." It added, "Current views are by far the worst of Barack Obama's presidency." (18)

What happened?

From to 2012 to 2013, American's perception of race relations took a dramatic downward turn and have steadily worsened since. I will suggest that our hard-working, Theory-wielding sociologists, intellectuals, journalists and Social Justice advocates, using their virulent new brand of Identity Politics that is rooted in cynical Postmodern Critical Race Theory, have contributed to our current cultural pessimism.

For the last decade, Americans have been ceaselessly and increasingly bombarded with the false and flimsy narrative that everything – *Everything!* – is about Systemic Racism (and secondarily, all associated 'isms'). We have been flooded with and now drowned in the idea that every social interaction is secretly laden with implicit, traumatic bias against an ever-increasing number of marginalized groups (people of color, women, the trans community, any non-cis sexual preference, etc). On page 73 of *White Fragility,* Ms. Diangelo informs us that "racism is the bedrock" of American society.

Race Forward (a group that "brings systemic analysis and an innovative approach to complex race issues") states on their website, "According to our research, U.S. media used the words "systemic racism" more in June 2020 than in the previous 30 years combined." (19)

In 2020, with Critical Race Theory based Social Justice themes prominently displayed in college and professional sports, one third of usual viewers began watching less. (20)

CORRELATION IS NOT CAUSATION.

Pause again here to remember that, just because educated people tell you that something is a fact does not make it a fact. Ms. Diangelo might be a sincere member the Cult of Critical Theory. This does not mean that other intelligent people must also believe. In fact, if you consider yourself an intelligent person, you should ceaselessly weigh the merit of the information you receive. Ask for evidence. Think for yourself. Decide on your own.

It is always sloppy thinking to assume that any correlation equates to causation. That is, if two things seem related, don't assume that one caused the other. Just because it seems to rain every time I plan a picnic does not mean my picnics affect the weather. I might be able to make a plausible case that the caustic babble spewed by scholars and activists has polluted our common discourse. But in the absence of factual evidence, I cannot prove it. I am suggesting strong correlation, but not direct causation (though I personally believe it to be true).

It is the same as if you were charged with a murder and I am the prosecuting attorney. I might lay out a very plausible case that sounds true. But if I have no factual evidence, you must go free. It is my duty to prove guilt and not your duty to prove innocence. Theory does the opposite. It assumes that a guilty hierarchy is in place and leaves the 'oppressors' to beg for their innocence. We'll return to this idea later.

The false narratives of Critical Race Theory play out in the media daily. With some understanding of current Sociology and Social Justice activism, we'll examine various cases. In each, I'll attempt to present factual evidence to demonstrate how and where false narratives have been slyly (or overtly) inserted. Some of the cases will be very high-profile, others more obscure. But every case has been politicized by those who would force feed us their incessant perversion of truth.

CHAPTER TWO.

THE FRAGILE LOGIC BEHIND WHITE FRAGILITY.

PLEASE NOTE:

Again, this book seeks to uproot the false narratives that have crept into public discourse. This chapter specifically challenges one of the more blatant and provocative peddlers of Critical Race Theory. Ms. Robin Diangelo ascribes malignant racial bias to all White actions and thoughts and even to family values and any sense of nostalgia. I believe she is wrong, and that Critical Race Theory promotes social illness.

An argument against Ms. Diangelo's charged racial rhetoric is *not* an argument against People of Color or a negation of the very real issues they face.

That stated, let's move ahead...

THE INHERENT PESSIMISM OF THEORISTS.

A better subtitle for Robin Diangelo's *White Fragility: Why it's so Hard for White People to Talk About Racism* would be, *Why it's so Hard for White People to Talk About Racism with Me Personally, Robin Diangelo.*

Let's explore that.

Ms. Diangelo opens her book by showing that, like most adherents to Theory, she is deeply invested in America's tragic past. The second, third and fourth sentences of her Author's Note demonstrate America's vile nature. These mention the attempted genocide of indigenous North Americans, the enslavement of

Africans and struggle of women to secure voting rights, respectively.

But why? The Foreword has already doused the Reader in pessimism. Race is "a disease. A card. A plague. Original sin." Whiteness has been likened to the literal Devil, capital D, while the author is aligned with "evangelicals." Whiteness is the "nemesis" of democracy and truth.

In this same first paragraph of the Author's Note she claims that "any gains we have made thus far [since our Nation's founding] have come through identity politics." As stated previously, Identity Politics was a term coined in the 1977 and is deeply rooted in Critical Theory. Classic American liberal thinkers did not utilize Theory's 'frameworks of oppression' or Identity Politics' 'intersecting levels of trauma' when they banned the international slave trade in 1808 or ratified the Fifteenth Amendment in 1870.

Ms. Diangelo retroactively and incorrectly applies the modern notion of Identity Politics to events that predate it by decades and centuries. Yes, those people had identities and yes, they engaged in politics, but they were not Critical Race Theorists. I suspect this misapplication was done to give Identity Politics more unearned worth and weight with current Readers (Readers who have likely *not* previously studied the philosophical constructs already discussed here). Assuming that Ms. Diangelo has studied these constructs, her misapplication here already begins to undercut her credibility.

Why open a book with such a flood of negativity and misinformation? The answer is that Critical Race Theory and Identity Politics are rooted in negativity and require a sullen soil riddled with strife in order to survive. These are schools of thought that literally and constantly read oppression into all means of discourse.

Recall the summary of Mr. Emmanuel Cannady's focus of study in Notre Dame's Sociology Department. "Emmanuel's research deals broadly with race and ethnicity, trauma, racialization" and "His main research agenda interrogates the racialized meanings of interpersonal interactions across different contexts..."

The modus operandi of Theory-minded sociologists is to 'problematize and reify.' 'Reify' means 'to make real.' These sociologists like to 'reify' things, perhaps because they spend so much time playing make-believe. Sociologists create new problems, demonstrate how they inflict trauma (ideally intersecting traumas) and make them real. The rest of us lack the divine ability to simply think things into being (Sorry, I slipped into opinion mode).

For example, any female or Person of Color can be physically attracted to any other person. But with Critical Race Theory, if a White male is physically attracted to an Asian or Latino woman, he is 'fetishizing' them. That's a social trauma he inflicts upon them, even if neither party was aware of it.

If a White person acknowledges Black person's Blackness, they are traumatically 'racializing' that Black person. If that same White person does not acknowledge that same Black person's Blackness, they are traumatically 'centering' that Black person in Whiteness. It's an elegantly toxic and self-perpetuating Theory. But again, this Theory requires hate and failure in order to exist and metastasize.

THE 'PROOF' OF SYSTEMIC RACISM.

Let's move out of the very first paragraph of the Author's Note and delve into the actual text.

Throughout *White Fragility*, Ms. Diangelo repeatedly demonstrates her devout belief in Critical Race Theory. She continuously uses phrases like "the system of racism" and the "dominance within the racial hierarchy" and "I understand racism as a system." All of these examples occur before the mid-way point of Chapter One. In Chapter Two she mentions "deeply internalized patterns of dominance and submission." Later in Chapter Three, "racism is a structure, not an event." All of this is pure Postmodern Critical Race Theory.

She believes in these invisible racial hierarchies. Her proof they exist? 'Other people say so.' She quotes like-minded Theorists throughout *White Fragility*.

Is there other proof? On page 32 Ms. Diangelo writes, "of the hundred top-grossing films worldwide in 2016, ninety-five were directed by white Americans."

Is this true?

No. No, it isn't.

The hundred top-grossing films worldwide in 2016 included the following ***twenty-five*** non-White directors (in no certain order):

1 - Steven Chow, Mei Ren Yu.

2 - Justin Lin, Star Trek Beyond.

3 - Zhang Yimou, The Great Wall.

4 - John M. Chu, Now You See Me 2.

5 - Makoto Shinkai, Kimi No Na Wa.

6 - James Wan, The Conjuring 2.

7 - Nitesh Tiwari, Dangal.

8 - Babak Najafi, London Has Fallen.

9 - Cheng Pou-Soi, Xi You Ji.

10 - Wong Jing, Du Cheng Yun 3.

11 - Dante Lam, Operation Mekong.

12 - Antoine Fuqua, The Magnificent Seven.

13 - Fede Alvarze, Don't Breath.

14 - Daniel Lee, Time Raiders.

15 - Tim Story, Ride Along 2.

16 - Yibai Zhang, I Belong to You.

17 - Xiao Lu Xue, Finding Mr. Right 2.

18 - Miao Yue, Da Hou Zhong.

19 - Lok Man Leung, Cold War 2.

20 - Shen ding, Railroad Tigers.

21 - Song Xiaofei, Some Like it Hot.

22 - Jennifer Nelson, Kung Fu Panda 3.

23 - Jazz Boon, Line Walker.

24 - Chun Zhang, Da yo Hai Tang.

25 - Sang-ho Yeon, Train to Busan.

Not only is Ms. Diangelo's claim here blatantly wrong when one examines it factually (I went through all one hundred), the argument it makes is anecdotal (that is, not based on systematic science) at best. And even anecdotally, it makes no sense.

Again, consider the famed Black economist Thomas Sowell when he stated, "Capitalism knows only one color: that color is green; all else is necessarily subservient to it, hence, race, gender and ethnicity cannot be considered within it." Showbusiness is a business. Anyone who can help turn a profit will get the work. Again, we see People of Color (including Asian people, the unwanted stepchildren of Critical Race Theory) negating Ms. Diangelo's assertions.

Ms. Diangelo argues that people are constantly 'socialized' into 'group memberships' as we experience the world around us. This process teaches us what we are (sex, race, physical traits, personal ability or lack thereof) and what we are not. The socialized 'lens' that we view our world through is necessary because, "Without it, a person could not function in any human society." She does not add that this basic truism has applied to every society that has ever existed.

She then argues against "individualism," classically defined by the qualities of autonomy, personal industry, independent free will, self-reliance and the freedom to act ungoverned by an oppressive central authority. Ms. Diangelo states that our individualist notions make us feel artificially unaffected by 'group membership.' As individuals, we feel group membership has no bearing on our individual opportunity or success.

But "opportunity is not equally distributed across race, class or gender" (page 10). This is another basic truism that also applies to every society that has ever existed on earth. Consider India's caste system. Consider the dismal plight of today's women and homosexuals in the Middle East and Africa. In both places, homosexuality is still criminalized in most of these regions and in some places is punishable by death. Consider the current Chinese Muslims being forcibly detained and 'reeducated.' Consider the existing slave trade in Africa. Consider the fine people of West Virginia.

Disparities between groups has been the age-old rule of society since mankind became bipedal, not the exception. Modern America arguably comes closest to the unattainable idea of absolute equality.

Individualism, says Ms. Diangelo, makes Whites believe that they have earned their success when, in her reality, it is accrued via the privilege and "unearned advantages" of Whiteness. She argues that this racial ignorance makes it difficult for Whites to pause and consider their privilege.

Whites, she argues, also need to abandon any sense of complete objectivity and acknowledge their inherent racial bias. Everyone has unfounded preconceptions (bias) about other races. We must be aware of and account for bias. To ignore this bias is to proceed with blinders that limit your view of racial reality.

These two ideas – acknowledging the limits of both individualism and objectivity – are entirely proper. But these apply universally to everyone, everywhere. They are not unique to modern 'Whiteness.' Acknowledging the limitations of *any* idea is wise. Ms. Diangelo cannot seem to grasp the limitations of Critical Race Theory, Systemic Racism and Identity Politics. Each one is a limited idea, not a fact, and they're not even very *good* ideas.

On page 16, Ms. Diangelo cites an article by Thomas Jefferson. She argues that, mindful of the "enormous economic interests in justifying enslavement," Jefferson looked for scientific evidence of Black inferiority. She implies that Thomas Jefferson sought to advance slavery.

Jefferson's article defends itself against close scrutiny by its length, its great density of topics and its rambling nature. But, if one reads the document (2), as I did, you see the truth. Jefferson was actually musing on possible genetic differences between Blacks and Whites and how these might affect a free, post-emancipation society.

In this same article, Jefferson states, "In the very first session held under the republican government, the assembly passed a law for the perpetual prohibition of the importation of slaves. This will in some measure stop the increase of this great political and moral evil, while the minds of our citizens may be ripening for a complete emancipation of human nature."

Jefferson also wrote, "emancipate all slaves born after passing the act" and have freed slaves "brought up, at the public expence, to tillage, arts or sciences, according to their geniusses, till the females should be eighteen, and the males twenty-one years of age, when they should be colonized to such place as the circumstances of the time should render most proper, sending them out with arms, implements of houshold and of the handicraft arts, seeds, pairs of the useful domestic animals, and to declare them a free and independent people, and extend to them our alliance and protection."

It is extremely clear that Thomas Jefferson was working to *end* slavery. Ms. Diangelo's assertion that Jefferson intended to justify and perpetuate slavery is an absolute falsehood. It is either an act of scholarly ineptitude or deceit. Either way, still more of her credibility slips away.

Ms. Diangelo is at her best when she discusses basic, universal truisms. For example, on page 19 she lays out a viable and acceptable definition of 'prejudice.' Prejudice, she argues, is pre-judgement. Prejudice is any preconception of a person or cultural group based on limited information and shared assumptions. A White male raised in rural Indiana (as I was) might have negative preconceptions of urban Blacks. An urban, northern Black might have negative preconceptions of a rural southern White person adorned in tattered overalls and Confederate flags. A Latino might have positive preconceptions of Asians. These examples are mine, not Ms. Diangelo's.

Ms. Diangelo states that we all have these preconceptions, or prejudices, and that they are not intrinsically bad. She argues that pre-judging is necessary to help us form a workable concept of the world around us in order for us to function in society. She adds that anyone who claims not to operate with these preconceptions is demonstrating "a profound lack of self-awareness." All of this is a very pragmatic way to consider how we experience our personal environment.

Ms. Diangelo is careful to state that her definition of pre-judging here should not be confused with the more common understanding of 'prejudice' that implies moral failure.

On page 20 she defines 'discrimination' as action based on prejudice. One has to assume she means *harmful* action as she leaves this out of her definition. Scholars like Thomas Sowell have more complete and nuanced definitions of discrimination. Ms. Diangelo adds that discrimination can range from overt violence to subtle avoidance and that "everyone has prejudice, and everyone discriminates."

There is no fault or flaw in any of these ideas about prejudice and discrimination. But these ideas exist *outside of* Critical Race Theory. When Ms. Diangelo next attempts to graft these viable ideas onto the diseased trunk of Critical Race Theory, she begins to fail. Sadly, she does this before the end of page 20 where she states, "When a group's collective prejudice is backed by the power of legal authority and institutional control, it is transformed into racism, a far-reaching system that functions independently from the intentions or self-images of individual actors." This is Critical Race Theory's essence.

PROJECTING RACE ONTO EVERTHING.

A plausible case is not proof of causation. Ms. Diangelo might paint some pretty word pictures, but when the canvas is turned sideways it is still two-dimensional. Her analysis clings to and is confined within Critical Race Theory.

In her third chapter, Ms. Diangelo discusses the 'new racism,' a highly adaptable and always invisible monster that eludes social progress and thus keeps her foolish and unsupported notions relevant. She points to Martin Luther King Jr. when he stated that one day people would be judged by their character and not by the color of their skin. Ms. Diangelo then asserts that White people grabbed this and intentionally twisted it into an 'easy out.' She seems to apply this to all White people, equally, invariably, universally and everywhere.

According to Ms. Diangelo, White people simply decided not to 'see' the color of people's skin and therefore they (White people) could not be racist. That such an educated person could make such an ignorant claim is amazing. But, as dictators and despots throughout the ages have known, the uninformed masses will often spot the small lies while falling for the Big Lie. Critical Race Theory is the Big Lie.

Of course, no White person *literally* ceased noticing the physical attributes of those they encountered. Many did embrace Dr. King's message. Many did begin very consciously setting aside any 'socialized' preconceptions and attempted to gauge each individual by their character. And progress was made.

On page 59, Ms. Diangelo states that it is racist to remember "the good old days." Recalling the past with a sense of nostalgia, no matter how vaguely, is literally a racist act. Nearly all people, everywhere, at some point in their lives, have longed for a simpler prior time, even a time they never experienced. She produces a laundry list of past events (enslavement, rape, genocide, lynchings, etc.) as if to prove the past was somehow universally unsalvageable. She actually states that "a romanticized past is strictly a white construct."

So that we avoid an argument of semantics, I'll define anything 'romanticized' as being overly amorous, idealized, fanciful or unrealistic. If you watched "The Last Dance," Michael Jordan clearly enjoyed reminiscing about his days on the court. Some in the series contradict Mr. Jordan's 'romanticized' accounts of those events. This one example shatters Ms. Diangelo's assertion, and more credibility falls away.

On page 61 Ms. Diangelo states that "romanticized 'traditional'" family values are also "racially problematic." Now, it must have taken great effort to find fault with 'traditional family values.' But again, this is a dedicated Cult member who has trained herself to see racial problems in *everything*. If traditional family values are problematic, Ms. Diangelo, which values do we turn to? (Please say 'Critical Theory vales.' I would love that debate.)

On page 72, Ms. Diangelo states, "Racism is a systemic, societal, institutional, omnipresent and epistemologically embedded phenomenon the pervades every vestige of our reality." This is hardly necessary, given the preceding 71 pages. But it does reinforce her solid belief in the stark framework of Critical Race Theory. She writes on the same page, "If we cannot discuss these dynamics or see ourselves within them, we cannot stop participating in racism."

We need to talk about *her* Critical Race Theory dynamics on *her* terms. If we push beyond Critical Race Theory – this one narrow way of viewing society - or, worse still, if we state that we don't subscribe to it, we are racists who are retreating into White Supremacy. That is her primary failure. She has an inability or unwillingness to see beyond the limited scope of her so-called expertise.

On page 82, "racism is a social system embedded in the culture and its institutions." Therefore, "your parents could not have taught you not to be racist, and your parents could not have been free of racism themselves." Furthermore, most parents only teach their children "not to admit to prejudice." This is all part of "the socialization process and the inescapable dynamics of human culture."

These are broad and hefty generalizations. But, as Ms. Diangelo wrote on page 12, "I am quite comfortable generalizing." Again, she assumes that all White people are identically socialized and have identical cultures. She underscores (again) the inherent pessimism of Theorists. She does hint at the power of "culture," a notion that remains vague and unexplored.

"Every vestige of our reality" is completely permeated by racism, she argues. Racism is "embedded in the culture." Such binary, all-or-none statements certainly resonate with the unquestioning congregation of faithful Critical Race Theory zealots (and help to sell her book). But what about those who value rational and independent thought?

Because these are not factual statements, Ms. Diangelo cannot 'prove' them, and I cannot 'disprove' them. But we can debate their intellectual merits.

To claim that any single thing colors 'every aspect of all reality' is to claim omnipotent knowledge. This is, of course, impossible. I am familiar with my reality, but I still have preconceptions. Ms. Diangelo has already stated these preconceptions are universal and necessary. She says that to deny preconceptions is to show an extreme lack of self-awareness. She argues, essentially, that none of us can know everything. I certainly lack such omnipotence.

Ms. Diangelo implies that she, with her PhD in Sociology, is fully aware of and has explored "every vestige of our reality" and found racism within. While I cannot make such a bold claims, being merely mortal, I can suggest that her ego has far, far surpassed her reason. She again loses credibility.

Chapter six, "Anti-Blackness," begins on page 89. It states that all White people harbor "deep guilt about what we have done and what we continue to do; the unbearable knowledge of our complicity in the profound torture of black people from past to present." She continues, "I believe that the white collective fundamentally hates blackness for what it reminds us of: that we are capable and guilty of perpetrating immeasurable harm and that our gains come through the subjugation of others."

These are heavy charges. Let me offer an opposing view. Just as we should not impose our current norms on past figures, we should not shackle our current generation to past failures.

As protests raged in the summer of 2020, many protestors toppled statues of important historical figures (I'll keep referring to them as protestors, but in using mob violence to destroy public property they became vandals, if not outright rioters). Those who toppled the statues were projecting our current cultural understandings upon those figures from the past. It was as if George Washington and Winston Churchill should have somehow escaped the "socialization process and the inescapable dynamics of human culture" that Ms. Diangelo has acknowledged. The protestors seemed to believe that those bygone figures should have somehow predicted and lived by our current cultural norms.

This, of course, is impossible. Like all of us, these were flawed people. They did great things in the context of the cultural norms of their time. It is both unwise and unfair to project our current norms onto them. To set this precedent means that we will all be toppled by our descendants. Whatever good we might do today will be negated by the posthumous 'crimes' charged against us.

In the same way, it is unwise and unfair to perpetually tie current people to the crimes committed in the past. How long must Germans carry the heavy guilt of the Jewish Holocaust? How long should Rwandans feel shame for the 1994 genocidal slaughter of Tutsi and Hutu peoples? How far into the future should remorse burden the citizens of the Democratic Republic of Congo for 2002's so-called Cleaning the Slate of the Bambuti? These people were considered 'subhuman' by the majority. And, perhaps more importantly, who gets to decide?

In my work as a physician (a Hospitalist), I see a broad range of individuals. Most are average people who struggle to get through the next month or the next week or even the next day. People whose main worries are rent payments, substance abuse, maintaining a marriage, living on a pension, etc. People who, despite their limitations and life's constant adversities, try to live a simple, decent lives. These are people with no additional resources to weigh their existential complicity in remote subjugations or the crimes attributed to some invisible philosophical framework. In short, the average American is too preoccupied with just getting by to wallow in Ms. Diangelo's deep guilt, unbearable knowledge and fundamental hatred.

On page 109, Ms. Diangelo wrote, "in 2016 the Oscars were challenged for their lack of diversity...for failing to nominate a single black actor for a second year in a row." She quoted actress Helen Mirren as stating, "It just so happened it went that way." When pressed about this two-year drought of diversity, Ms. Mirren said "it's unfair to attack the academy." Ms. Diangelo wrote that this showed how "pointing out white advantage will often trigger patterns of confusion, defensiveness, and righteous indignation."

It is true that the Oscars had no Black nominees in its four acting categories in 2015 and 2016. But in the eleven years including 2006 to 2016, there were eighteen Black nominees representing **41%** of all nominees in these four acting categories. From 2006 to 2020 (inclusive), Black actors represented a full **50%** all nominees. Black Americans represented about 13% of the population during these years. Ms.

Mirren was right to defend the academy against suggestions of racism.

Ms. Diangelo's assertion of 'white superiority' in this example seems very fragile. She turned an anomaly into a false narrative while discreetly (purposefully?) ignoring the broader truth. Her credibility as a thoughtful scholar and author again suffers.

PUSHING BEYOND CRITICAL THEORY.

When I was sixteen, I spent a summer pruning Christmas trees. Our crew would use slender, 14-inch knives to sculpt the trees into their desired conical shape. It was the worst job I ever had. It was a summer of sunburns, bug bites, sweat, pine sap, blisters and band aids. For the next six months I couldn't look at a pine tree without seeing its asymmetry and annoying irregular branches. All I could see were the conifers' imperfections.

Ms. Diangelo has spent a career scrutinizing race. It is unsurprising that, like my pine trees, she sees charged, racialized issues everywhere she looks. Ms. Diangelo's arguments are anchored in the single variable of race. Her assumptions are anchored in race. Her conclusions are drawn through the single, narrow lens of race. Whiteness is assumed guilty and must prove its innocence.

Throughout her book, she operates under the inflexible set of faulty assumptions discussed earlier. The socialized preconceptions of Whiteness are inherently negative, essentially identical and unchanging through time. White people lack the 'racial stamina' to acknowledge, analyze, understand, challenge and change (or even temporarily suspend) such preconceptions.

She ignores the enormous, indelible and ever-increasing stamp of influence made by People of Color on American 'systems' and our shared culture. She largely dismisses the White allies who fought for and are fighting for an equal and shared humanity for all. Instead, racism is a monstrous, monolithic system that "becomes the default of the society and is reproduced automatically."

White Fragility argues that oppressive systems begin with ideologies that are constantly reinforced in every means of discourse and that social penalties inhibit us from challenging such ideologies. This, of course, is the paradigm of Postmodern Critical Race Theory that she would have you adopt. She wants you to believe her oppressive ideology and adopt her means of discourse.

Again, liberal thought is the very contradiction to Critical Theory. Liberal thought entails constant challenges to ideas and ideologies. Liberal thinkers of every culture and color created America and guided it through every step of its amazing evolution.

What happens when we employ liberal thought to investigate Ms. Diangelo's assumptions? More importantly, why hasn't she done so herself? Thomas Sowell once wrote, "There are certain possibilities that many among the intelligentsia cannot even acknowledge as possibilities, much less try to test empirically, which would be risking their whole vision of the world and of themselves." (1)

Ms. Diangelo seems to believe that all White people have "a limited worldview, a reliance on deeply problematic depictions of people" with an "internalized superiority" (page 37) that lead to a belief that is "so internalized, so submerged, that it is never considered" (page 34). She might as well be writing about herself and her university-based associates who have been so insulated from reality.

But we can be braver and more informed than Ms. Diangelo. We can look at social inequality through other lenses. We can reframe the question in a historical context. We can reverse the argument. We can compare current American society to other current societies.

View the social disparities caused by racism from an economic perspective. It is enormously expensive to have a marginalized group that is relatively under-educated, under-skilled, under-employed and relatively less healthy. That group must be supported financially through vast system of costly social support programs. These programs can in turn de-incentivize some from gaining greater education, employment and autonomy. It is in everyone's best economic interest to raise up, educate and maximally employ such a marginalized group.

Fortunately, we can count numerous ways that our 'social and institutional powers' have attempted and are attempting to do this (with mixed and sometimes disastrous results). Consider the push for affordable housing for low-income and minority groups as one example.

Start with the Fair Housing Act of 1968 (a subset of the larger Civil Rights Act of 1968). Unlike the Civil Rights Act of 1866 which prohibited racial discrimination in housing, the 1968 Act provided official enforcement protections via the Federal Government. In short, the 1968 Act had teeth.

Dissatisfied with the Fair Housing Act, political organizers and leaders in the Democratic Party passed the Home and Mortgage Disclosure Act (HMDA) in 1975. These same players got the Community Reinvestment Act (CRA) passed in 1977, despite worries about its adverse effects on banking standards.

This allowed Left leaning activist groups like the Association of Community Organizers for Reform Now (ACRON) to apply political, legal and media pressure onto banks so that they would further relax their lending practices (note that Barak Obama gave legal representation to ACORN in 1995). A relaxation in banks' underwriting standards duly occurred, and in the 1980's banks got increased CRA credit by issuing so-called 'subprime loans.'

Democratic President Bill Clinton accelerated this process in the 1990's when he began his own crusade for affordable housing (despite failing miserably with the Good Faith Fund as Arkansas' governor). The Clinton Administration leveraged the full force and finances of the Justice Department to pressure banks even further, with aid from HUD Secretary Henry Cisneros and the NAACP.

Cisneros left HUD in 1997 and took a high-paying job on the board of subprime mortgage lender Countrywide. Cisneros was replaced as HUD Secretary by Andrew Cuomo, who aggressively pushed banks for even more credit leniency. Additionally, Cuomo secured no-money-down, no-closing cost mortgages for low-income and minority home buyers while authorizing payments to the brokers who pushed these high-risk loans. Otherwise stated, these brokers risked Justice Department punishment for not meeting quotas and also received Federally backed financial incentives to approve high-risk subprime loans. They got paid to peddle sub-prime loans.

Throughout this period, the Clinton team pressured banks to sell these high-risk loans to the 'secondary market' so that the banks would have more cash to create more high-risk loans. According to Peter Schweizer, "Subprime lending exploded during the Clinton years. It increased twenty-fold between 1993 and 2000." (2)

The government-related entities Fannie Mae and Freddie Mac both got busy buying up these subprime mortgages. During the Clinton years, Fannie Mae CEO James Johnson lowered the standard for loans that this agency would purchase. His successor in 1999, Franklin Raines, increased the goals for minority home ownership even further. Mortgage company Countrywide was one of Fannie and Freddie's biggest sources of subprime loans

Of course, we know how this story ends. The sub-prime mortgage industry collapsed in 2008 and millions of People of Color were financially devasted. This was forty years after the Fair Housing Act of 1968 and the present-day media's limited attention was on the so-called 'predatory lenders' who originated the high-risk loans. The attention was not on the career politicians who applied the pressure of the Federal Government on these lenders. Clinton, Cisneros, Cuomo and many others exited as multi-millionaires (or into comfortable and blameless private sector positions that would make them so).

Many current Social Justice activists cite the subprime mortgage crisis as yet another example of how People of Color are abused by 'the system.' Ms. Diangelo specifically mentions subprime mortgages on page 59 in a list of offenses that also includes genocide, mob violence and Jim Crow laws. But in truth it serves as an example of how high-minded and short-sighted Social Justice advocates push agendas can harm the people they want to help.

This example also shows a robust, sustained, decades-long (and monumentally expensive) attempt by 'the system' to help People of Color to become home owners. This single example refutes Ms. Diangelo's assumptions about Systemic Racism. And this is just *one* alternate lens to look through.

CONCLUSIONS.

It is likely that any current stagnation in racial progress and any worsening of race relations are at least in part due to books like *White Fragility* and the ruinous effects of Critical Race Theory.

Ms. Diangelo seems to base most of her assumptions on her interactions with other White people during her role as a workplace diversity consultant. She offers many anecdotes about these exchanges.

Ms. Diangelo fails to see what happens when she enters a diversity training session armed with her PhD level understanding of Theory. When she politely bestows upon her audience the knowledge that they are all racists in a self-perpetuating racist system, she expects "gratitude and relief" (page 4). But these unenlightened fools then dare to challenge Ms. Diangelo's orthodoxy and, in doing so, reveal their 'fragility.'

This is the fundamental failure with her understanding of her audience. She has spent a career taking one school of thought, Critical Race Theory, and 'reifying' it. *She* believes it is real and demands that everyone else take it as gospel. It's remarkable that a scholar with such insight would lack such insight.

This is not an indictment of all Sociologists and part-time philosophers. There are many doing good work, many who can still see above the choking smog of their colleagues' obtuse and arrogant meanderings. Perhaps some of these Sociologists will study the vast, stinking trash heap of Applied Postmodern Critical Race Theory and its noxious effects. Maybe they will be able to explain how so many bright people trapped themselves in mental birdcages.

CHAPTER THREE.
THE WOMAN WHO WOULD ASSASSINATE ABRAHAM LINCOLN. THE 1619 PROJECT.

"Anti-black racism runs in the very DNA of this country."

This theory, blatant and bare, appears near the halfway point of Mrs. Nikole Hanna-Jones lead article in her much discussed *The 1619 Project*. It is the central premise of her work. The tag line. The take away. But this naked theory needed dressing up to make it presentable.

Being intellectually bankrupt, Mrs. Hanna-Jones had to wrap *The 1619 Project* in tattered bits of history. These altered bits are taken out of context or stripped of context. What remains is certainly eloquent and, if you don't heavily fact check, persuasive. But it fails as both history and journalism because it takes such grand liberties with the truth of our shared, broad, tumultuous American story.

If you read it, you'll likely sense that there's something missing in *The 1619 Project*. It is an extraordinarily limited narrowing of American history. It is a forced perspective not unlike that used by film makers in order to trick the viewer (or in this case, the Reader) into believing that which cannot be true. It is a Social Justice warrior's passion project that stumbles over its contrivances and its overt hostility to and stereotyping of 'White America.'

If you don't believe there's subtle anger here, read Mrs. Hanna-Jones' letter to Notre Dame's student newspaper in 1995 for an example of her overt anger. "The white race is the biggest murderer, rapist, pillager, and thief in the modern world...Christopher Columbus and those like him were no different then Hitler...can only be described as acts of the devil...these savage people pump drugs and guns into the Black community...continue to be bloodsuckers..." (1)

What historical liberties did Mrs. Hanna-Jones take?

As stated previously, there was no 'America' in 1619. The colonists in North America were thoroughly and legally British. Slaves arrived on British ships to service British business ventures that forwarded products and revenues back across the Atlantic. It would take 160 years before British colonists formed an 'American' identity stable enough to severe those ties via the Declaration of Independence.

Ms. Hanna-Jones writes of the drafting of the Declaration of Independence, "At the time, one-fifth of the population within the 13 colonies struggled under a brutal system of slavery unlike anything that had existed in the world before."

It is true in that technical innovations allowed North American slaves different modes of travel and toil and that these slaves were in a new geographical location. But to imply that it was uniquely brutal is not supported by history.

The known history of the African continent is unfortunately ripe with pre-colonial slave trading, forced labor and sexual bondage. The pharaohs of Ancient Egypt enslaved workers who built the pyramids. Evidence shows that Egyptian slaves who laid the 2.5-tonne granite blocks making up the pyramids died with deformed bones and broken limbs. By some estimates, up to one million slaves died making the Great Wall in China. Slavery in India escalated during the Muslim domination of northern India after the 11th-century. When Aztec noblemen died, they were cremated with forty slaves, 20 women and 20 men. And an estimated 400,000 slaves died for bloody sport within the walls Rome's ancient Coliseum.

The Arab Slave Trade is rarely discussed but should be remembered. It started in the seventh century as Islam gained strength in North Africa. It would last for over a thousand years (and still continues in some ways today). Arab Muslims bought or captured Africans and sold them in the Middle East. The African slaves who guarded harems guards were often castrated.

Slavery existed nearly everywhere in Africa before these Islamic invaders arrived. In central East Africa, "ethnic groups such as the Yao, Makua and Marava were fighting against each other and entire peoples within the continent traded with people they had captured through wars." (2) Having no prison system, conquering African tribes simply sold excess captives to other African tribes. The arriving Arab Muslims discovered preexisting slave trading operations, which facilitated their purchase of slaves. "Scientific research concludes that about three out of four slaves died before they reached the market where they were to be sold." (2) Some estimate the Arab Slave Trade far surpassed the Atlantic Slave Trade in the total number of captives transported out of Africa. Why is this not being discussed? Religious solidarity. "There are 500 million Muslims in Africa, and it is better to blame the West than talk about the past crimes of Arab Muslims." (2)

While exact numbers are impossible to gather, the Arab Slave Trade took an estimated 9.85 million Africans from Africa to the Middle East. Another 4 million Africans were sold into the Persian Gulf and India. This continued into the early 20th century. (3)

Consider Dr. David Livingston, the Indiana Jones of British Abolitionists in the 19th century. He witnessed firsthand the Arab Slave Trade in Africa. His diary entries capture some of the most barbaric and inhumane practices ever recorded as African men, women and children were shackled and marched for weeks toward ports. There they were crammed into ships set for Middle Eastern Muslim nations.

We should remember and we should discuss slavery in America. Like the Jewish Holocaust, to ignore it or to forget it would risk the hard and painful lessons learned from it. But slavery and genocide continue today.

Consider that, in 2018, the African continent recorded the highest rate of modern-day enslavement in the world. (4)

In modern day Mauritania, the practice of slavery remains deeply entrenched, where a slave's status is inherited. These enslaved people cannot own land or inherit possessions. Those enslaved are darker-skinned Haratin and their owners are the lighter-skinned Moors. (5)

Today in the Central African Republic, armed groups don't simply commit sexual violence and enslavement as a byproduct of fighting. It is a tactic of war. Commanders don't just condone the rapes and sexual enslavement committed by their forces. In some cases order it or commit it themselves. (6)

Slavery was a constant for countless millennia. It existed in every culture and at all times (including today). What is unusual about American 'Whiteness' and slavery is not that is existed, but that Whites fought for it to end. The very idea of 'America' nearly ended during the bitter and bloody Civil War that lead to emancipation.

These examples do not and can never excuse The United States' shameful history of slavery, but they do underscore mankind's inherent flaws in all cultures and in every era. America's slavery experience is, sadly, not an isolated occurrence of an odious practice that permeates history and continues in many forms today. And this brief account of slavery in no way is meant to diminish the very real and current effects of slavery on Black Americans. It serves only to broaden our perspective.

Therefore, if the United States was 'built' on slavery, then so was much of China, India, the Muslim world in the Middle East and Africa itself. Of course, to claim that any of these vast and complicated areas could be built on any single concept or practice is a gross oversimplification.

The Cult of Critical Theory needs such oversimplifications (as we shall see in the numerous examples that follow throughout this book) because their arguments cannot support precise definitions, insightful debate or thoughtful challenges. 'Systems of oppression' are too vague to be exactly defined. If they can't be defined, they can't be debated. If they can't be debated, it can't be negated. That is the slippery, sly elegance of Critical Theory when wielded by cunning Sociologists and Social Justice warriors.

Mrs. Hanna-Jones stated, "...one of the primary reasons the colonists decided to declare their independence from Britain was because they wanted to protect the institution of slavery."

This statement is pure fantasy. Abolitionists had been present since slaves first appeared on North American soil, and anti-slavery sentiments grew in tandem in the American colonies and in Britain simultaneously. But it was Britain's strangulation of the colonist's economic and civic liberties that lead to the Declaration in 1776. Points of conflict included taxation, frontier policy, issues of immigration and naturalization, the lack of an effective and independent judiciary, excess bureaucracy, the presence of a British army on colonial soil and limitations on international trade, among many others.

There is no historical evidence that North American colonists defected from Britain in order to preserve slavery.

Mrs. Hanna-Jones argued that Thomas Jefferson, in his original draft of the Declaration of Independence, "tried to argue that it [slavery] wasn't the colonists' fault. Instead, he blamed the king of England for forcing the institution of slavery on the unwilling colonists and called the trafficking in human beings a crime."

Many North American colonies were started as business ventures or "charter companies" by British investors. These charters required approval by Britain's King. It is conceivable that slave-owning British businessmen demanded that their colonial underlings employ slave labor to save costs. And again, in the early 17th Century, the colonists were still British in law and culture.

Also, Jefferson never attempted to 'shift blame' for slavery, as Mrs. Hanna-Jones implied. Jefferson actually wrote, "he [the King] has waged cruel war against human nature itself, violating it's most sacred rights of life & liberty in the persons of a distant people who never offended him, captivating & carrying them into slavery in another hemisphere...determined to keep open a market where MEN should be bought & sold, he has prostituted his negative for suppressing every legislative attempt to prohibit or to restrain this execrable commerce."

This was one of about twenty charges Jefferson leveled against Britain at that time.

Mrs. Hanna-Jones wrote of an August 14, 1862, meeting between Abraham Lincoln and five free Black men. At issue was whether or not these Black representatives felt that repatriation to Africa (or South America) was viable.

Nikole Hanna-Jones wrote, "The Civil War had been raging for more than a year, and black abolitionists, who had been increasingly pressuring Lincoln to end slavery, must have felt a sense of great anticipation and pride."

On its surface, this is a harmless and truthful statement. But here, as throughout her paper, the author intentionally disregards the White American abolitionists who had been pressuring leaders since slaves first appeared centuries before. Again, the history of American abolitionism is too long and detailed for this discussion, but after Rhode Island passed legislation attempting to ban slavery in 1652, both White and Black Americans fought ceaselessly to end slavery.

In 1835 alone, Northern Abolitionists mailed over a million pieces of anti-slavery literature to the

South. There were about 16 million people in the US at that time, including about 2.5 million slaves. If just half of the 13.5 million those Whites lived in the South, then one in seven Southerners received anti-slavery mail in 1835. Of course, many of those 6.75 million Southerners would have been children, so the proportion of adults receiving abolitionist information was even greater.

She continued, writing that, "He [Lincoln] believed that free black people were a "troublesome presence" incompatible with a democracy intended only for white people. "Free them, and make them politically and socially our equals?" he had said four years earlier. "My own feelings will not admit of this; and if mine would, we well know that those of the great mass of white people will not.""

This record of Lincoln's thoughts 'four years earlier,' when read in its entirety, is clearly a rhetorical argument the great man had with himself. He pondered several ways to end slavery and measured their possible conflicts.

In this same document, Lincoln clearly said that Blacks deserved justice and human sympathy and that "those who deny it and make mere merchandise of him [Black people] deserve kickings, contempt and death."

Lincoln added in this document, "What I do say is that no man is good enough to govern another man without that other's consent. I say this is the leading principle, the sheet-anchor of American republicanism."

He also stated, "Slavery is founded in the selfishness of man's nature, opposition to it in his love of justice."

Finally, Lincoln stated, "Repeal the Missouri Compromise. Repeal all compromises. Repeal the Declaration of Independence. Repeal all history. You still cannot repeal human nature. It still will be the abundance of man's heart that slavery extension is wrong."

All these Lincoln passages are from the same document cited *very selectively* by Mrs. Hanna-Jones. This intentional distortion of one of the world's greatest statesmen is an insult to every thinking person.

In one of her most outrageous perversions of history, Mrs. Hanna-Jones wrote, "And now Lincoln was blaming them [Black people] for the war." She offers the passage, "Although many men engaged on either side do not care for you one way or the other . . . without the institution of slavery and the colored race as a basis, the war could not have an existence," the president told them.""

Read that again. According to Nikole Hanna-Jones, Abraham Lincoln, the Great Emancipator, blamed Black people for slavery and for the war over slavery.

Once again, when considering the full account, Readers understand that Lincoln was not blaming Black people for the war. He was lamenting that, were it not for the divisive issue of slavery, there would not be a war. In this same conversation Lincoln stated, "Your [Black] race are suffering, in my judgment, the greatest wrong inflicted on any people," and later,

"You are intelligent, and know that success does not as much depend on external help as on self-reliance."

Mrs. Hanna-Jones closes her statements about that Lincoln meeting with: "As Lincoln closed the remarks, Edward Thomas, the delegation's chairman, informed the president, perhaps curtly, that they would consult on his proposition. "Take your full time," Lincoln said. "No hurry at all.""

She seems to imply that Lincoln saw no urgency in this matter. But what she did not write was that, moments prior, Lincoln said, ""I want you [the free Blacks] to let me know whether this can be done or not. This is the practical part of my wish to see you. These are subjects of very great importance, worthy of a month's study, [instead] of a speech delivered in an hour."

Lincoln did not want a hurried opinion. He wanted a fully considered opinion.

Upon the conclusion of the Civil War, per Mrs. Hanna-Jones, "the formerly enslaved did not take up Lincoln's offer to abandon these lands." In arguing that Black people wished to remain on American soil she wrote, "Black Americans had long called for universal equality and believed, as the abolitionist Martin Delany said, "that God has made of one blood all the nations that dwell on the face of the earth.""

Here Mrs. Hanna-Jones misrepresents another historical figure. Martin Delany dreamed of establishing a Black settlement in West Africa. He visited Liberia, a United States colony founded by the American Colonization Society. He argued that Blacks had no future in the United States and suggested Black people should leave and found a new nation elsewhere.

And now we arrive at the very heart of Mrs. Hanna-Jones article. "Anti-black racism runs in the very DNA of this country, as does the belief, so well articulated by Lincoln, that black people are the obstacle to national unity."

Here she again deliberately distorts Abraham Lincoln's consistent message across the years that *slavery*, that vile institution that he hated and abolished, was the obstacle to national unity. Lincoln openly acknowledged the bigotry and animosity that many White people directed and would continue to direct at their Black neighbors. But nowhere did Lincoln blame Black people for this.

Mrs. Hanna-Jones wrote, "Faced with this unrest, the federal government decided that black people were the cause of the problem and that for unity's sake, it would leave the white South to its own devices. In 1877, President Rutherford B. Hayes, in order to secure a compromise with Southern Democrats that would grant him the presidency in a contested election, agreed to pull federal troops from the South."

Here Mrs. Hanna-Jones reduces the intricately complex and highly volatile political, economic, and societal problems surrounding the contested 1876 election and its aftermath to the sole issue that fits her agenda: "Black people were the cause of the problem."

Again, historical facts are not on her side.

Prior to his election, President Hayes had been a lawyer and staunch Abolitionist. He had defended refugee slaves in court during the antebellum years.

79

Facing a Democrat controlled Congress, President Hayes' efforts to protect the rights of southern Blacks were largely ineffective. This Democratic Congress tried to repeal the **Enforcement Acts**, which had been used to suppress **White supremacy groups**. Hayes, determined to protect Black voting rights, vetoed the Democrats' effort four times. The voting rights laws remained in effect, but the funds to enforce them were withheld by Congress.

In his diary, Hayes wrote, "My task was to wipe out the color line, to abolish sectionalism, to end the war and bring peace. To do this, I was ready to resort to unusual measures and to risk my own standing and reputation within my party and the country." All his efforts were in vain.

Near the end of her article, Mrs. Hanna-Jones wrote, "White America dealt with this inconvenience by constructing a savagely enforced system of racial apartheid that excluded black people almost entirely from mainstream American life — a system so grotesque that Nazi Germany would later take inspiration from it for its own racist policies."

To be sure, American segregation is an abysmal blight on our history. But there is no historical evidence that Nazi Germany took any lead from this. Hitler never traveled beyond Germany and Austria (save for brief forays, such as to a conquered Paris) and was famously ignorant of those in 'Der Ausland' (the entire world beyond Germany).

The great historical journalist William Shirer wrote that Hitler's fundamental ideals were formed during his twenties in Vienna and were never subsequently altered. Hitler's notions of Teutonic supremacy came from European philosophers Johann

Fitche, Georg Hegle, Heinrich Treitschke, Friedrich Nietzsche and from his own crackpot associates, primarily Alfred Rosenburg and Dietrich Eckart.

Hitler was influenced by the American Sociologists who spawned eugenics and was an admirer of Henry Ford's antisemitism. But again, no evidence exists that Hitler took note of racial segregation and unrest in the US.

To be sure, Black Americans have suffered and continue to suffer as our nation advances further from its past failures. Open, honest, factual conversations are part of this advancement. Sadly, Mrs. Nikole Hanna-Jones' divisive, dishonest rhetoric, supported not only by the New York Times but also a host of journalists and talk-show hosts, sabotages this process.

Unlike Robin Diangelo, who seems to sincerely suffer the ignorance of her own delusions of intellectual superiority, Mrs. Hanna-Jones appears to be a calculating hate-monger. She saw an opportunity to capitalize on America's collective angst. Hers is a work of callous journalistic deceit.

INTERLUDE.

The next few Chapters examine the factual details of several officer relates shootings. The goal in each case is to highlight the false narrative that was built up around it. In many cases, those who reinforce these false narratives do so using jargon specific to Critical Theory. Each false narrative has a political agenda (which should not be surprising since Critical

Theory is inherently both political and agenda driven).

These false narratives are very separate from the individual victims themselves. Each was a unique person with the same inherent worth as me or Robin Diangelo or you, the Reader. Each lived in circumstances that affected their view of the world and the choices they made. These are circumstances I have only experienced peripherally and briefly. My attempt to debase the false narratives applied to these unfortunate people is not an attack on them.

False narratives convince those who want to believe them. They convince a few who might sway either way. They convince very few who wait for (or dig for) facts. It is likely that a great, silent majority are left skeptical and suspicious. When the next tragic case arrives, perhaps a genuine case of racism in action, the impact is blunted by this doubt and cynicism.

I believe the vast majority of police are honorable men and women who serve their communities faithfully. False narratives unfairly malign those honorable police officers who have performed justly in tragic circumstances.

I also believe there are cases of police excess and individual officers who act on racist beliefs. False narratives cause many to either doubt the true merit of these cases or, in Social Justice fatigue, simply tune out.

Therefore, it benefits nearly* everyone to expose false narratives in favor of truth. (*Profiteering, power-hungry and publicity-minded politicians, activists, ournalists and scholars do not benefit. I'm okay with his).

CHAPTER FOUR.
ERIC GARNER.

On July 17, 2014, Police Officers Justin D'Amico and Daniel Pantaleo attempted to place Eric Garner under arrest. The officers were acting on orders to stop the sale of untaxed cigarettes in their precinct. These officers found Mr. Garner illegally selling loose, untaxed cigarettes. Their following interaction was captured on a cellphone video.

As the officers attempted to arrest Mr. Garner, he resisted both verbally and physically. Consequently, the officers were legally permitted to use "reasonable" physically force to effect Mr. Garner's arrest.

As Mr. Garner resisted arrest, Officer Pantaleo attempted two approved NYPD use of force tactics. The first involved an "arm bar." As the video made clear, Mr. Garner twisted his body and freed his arms, evaded Pantaleo's grasp, and avoided being placed in handcuffs.

Officer Pantaleo next attempted a second tactic called the "rear takedown" or "seat belt." There was nothing in the video to suggest that Officer Pantaleo intended or attempted to place Mr. Garner in a chokehold.

Investigators noted the significant difference in size and weight between Mr. Garner, who stood 6'2" and weighed close to 400 lbs., and Officer Pantaleo, who was considerably smaller. These investigators found that this disparity in size and weight clearly delayed Officer Pantaleo's ability to bring Mr. Garner under arrest quickly.

As Officer Pantaleo attempted to complete the rear takedown, the situation rapidly deteriorated. As Mr. Garner and Officer Pantaleo struggled, both men fell backward, slamming Pantaleo against a store window. In response to that collision, and to maintain a hold on Mr. Garner, Officer Pantaleo wrapped his left arm around Mr. Garner's neck, resulting in what was, in effect, a chokehold. Officer Pantaleo maintained that hold on Mr. Garner for a total of seven seconds. During the first few seconds of that hold, both men were falling to the sidewalk.

Mr. Garner did state, "I can't breathe," but investigators pointed out that he made this statement only *after* he fell to the sidewalk and *after* Officer Pantaleo released his grip from Mr. Garner's neck. There was no chokehold on Mr. Garner when he said he could not breathe, and no chokehold occurred after Mr. Garner he first said he could not breathe.

The media, despite having access to the same video seen by investigators and the general public, wove the false narrative of a sustained chokehold on the ground. Consider this line in an August 16' 2014 article from The Guardian - "Garner was being taken into custody for selling untaxed cigarettes, known as "loosies", when an officer put him in a chokehold and refused to let up, even as he gasped: "I can't breathe.""
(1)

At least two different medical experts explained that the sudden cardiac arrest suffered by Mr. Garner during this arrest could have had a number of causes other than the brief chokehold, including Mr. Garner's serious underlying medical conditions and severe morbid obesity. This was significant because it cast serious doubt on whether the chokehold itself contributed in any way Mr. Garner's death.

On December 3, 2014, the grand jury assigned to the case opted not to bring charges against the two officers.

The next day, US Attorney General Eric Holder stated, "the grand jury declined to return an indictment in this case. Now that the local investigation has concluded, I am here to announce that the Justice Department will proceed with a federal civil rights investigation into Mr. Garner's death.

This afternoon I spoke with the widow of Eric Garner to inform her and her family of our decision to investigate potential federal civil rights violations. I have been in touch with President Obama and Mayor de Blasio regarding our decision as well.

Our prosecutors will conduct an independent, thorough, fair and expeditious investigation." (2)

Mr. Holder added, "This is not a New York issue or a Ferguson issue alone. Those who have protested peacefully across our great nation following the grand jury's decision in Ferguson have made that clear."

Mr. Holder, speaking for the Obama Justice Department and reinforcing a false narrative, signaled to the protestors and the media that a racial injustice had occurred and would be rooted out. He said this despite contrary evidence and after a grand jury's decision. And he was, ultimately, proven wrong.

On December 4, 2014, President Obama stated that Eric Garner's case somehow, "speaks to the larger issues that we've been talking about now for the last week, the last month, the last year, and, sadly, for decades, and that is the concern on the part of too many minority communities that law enforcement is not working with them and dealing with them in a fair way." (3)

This was a calculated inference between Mr. Garner's decisions to engage in illegal activity and then forcefully resist arrest and ongoing racial issues. There was no evidence of any kind that Mr. Garner's arrest was racially motivated. Note that Mr. Garner had some thirty arrests prior to this last incident.

Because of the comments of prominent public figures and despite the findings of the grand jury, progressive scholars continued to press the blatantly false narrative of police abuse. The Fall, 2015, issue of Multicultural Education featured an article that stated, "In July 2014 in Staten Island a White police officer put an unarmed Black man [Eric Garner] in a chokehold and, despite the man's cries that he couldn't breathe, several New York Police Department officers continued to assault him until he died a few moments later." (4)

On July 16, 2019, The Department of Justice reported it would not bring criminal charges against the New York City police officer involved in the death of Eric Garner, citing "insufficient evidence."

"Let me say as clear and unequivocally as I can that Mr. Garner's death was a tragedy," Richard Donoghue, U.S. attorney for the Eastern District of New York, said at a news conference. "But these unassailable facts are separate and distinct from whether federal crime has been committed. And the evidence here does not support charging police Officer Daniel Pantaleo with a federal criminal civil rights violation." (5)

DISCUSSION.

There was no evidence to suggest that Garner's death was racially motivated. All evidence shows that he died, likely as the result of a heart attack, during a justifiable arrest in which he forcefully resisted. As of this writing, his case is still used as an example of 'systemic racism.'

CHAPTER FIVE.
MICHAEL BROWN.

These are the facts from the March 4, 2015, *United States Department of Justice Report Regarding the Criminal Investigation into the Shooting Death of Michael Brown by Ferguson, Missouri Police Officer Darren Wilson.* (1)

At approximately noon on Saturday, August 9, 2014, Officer Darren Wilson of the Ferguson Police Department ("FPD") shot and killed Michael Brown, an unarmed 18-year-old.

At approximately 11:53 a.m. on August 9, 2014, Brown and Witness 101 went to the 'Ferguson Market.' Surveillance video showed Brown stealing several packages of cigarillos and then forcefully shoving the store clerk who tried to stop him from leaving the store without paying. The clerk was about 5'6" and 150 lbs, while Brown was 6'5" and 289 lbs.

Brown again and aggressively moved toward the clerk. According to the store employees, Brown, looked "crazy" and said something like, "What are you gonna do about it?" Brown then exited the store and the clerk's daughter called 911.

Two toxicologists subsequently conducted blood and urine screens on samples collected from Brown's body. Brown tested positive for cannabinoids at levels consistent with Brown having ingested THC within a few hours before his death. This concentration of THC indicated that Brown, a known marijuana user, was likely intoxicated at the time he encountered Officer Wilson.

According to FPD records, at about 11:53 AM on August 9, 2014, a dispatcher called out a "stealing in progress" at the Ferguson Market. It described that the suspect's clothing and that they had stolen cigarillos. Officer Wilson heard this dispatch and the physical description of Brown.

Wilson was driving his cruiser when he approached Brown and his friend, 'Witness 101,' walking in the middle of the street. Wilson told the two men to walk on the sidewalk. Wilson suspected that Brown and Witness 101 were involved in the theft / assault at Ferguson Market based on the matching physical descriptions and the cigarillos in Brown's hands. Wilson called for backup, then positioned his cruiser in the street to block Brown and Witness 101.

Wilson attempted to open his driver's door, and said, "Hey, come here." Before Wilson got his leg out, Brown responded, "What the fuck are you gonna do?" Brown then slammed the door shut and Wilson told him to "get back." Wilson attempted to open the door again, telling Brown to, "Get the fuck back," but Brown pushed the door closed on Wilson a second time.

Wilson and other witnesses stated that Brown then reached into the cruiser through the open driver's window and began punching and grabbing Wilson. This was corroborated by bruising on Wilson's jaw and scratches on his neck, the presence of Brown's DNA on Wilson's collar, shirt, and pants, and Wilson's DNA on Brown's palm.

Leaning into the driver's window, with his arms and upper torso inside, Brown assaulted Wilson, "swinging wildly." Brown turned and handed the stolen cigarillos to Witness 101, then punched Wilson's jaw at least twice more.

Witness 103 was in his stopped truck immediately beside Wilson's cruiser. He would later state that he saw Brown punch Wilson at least three times in the face, through the open driver's window of the cruiser. Wilson was leaning back toward the passenger seat with his forearm up, trying to block the blows.

Wilson withdrew his gun and pointed it at Brown. Wilson warned Brown to stop or he was going to shoot him. Brown stated, "You are too much of a pussy to shoot," and used his right hand to seize

Wilson's gun. Brown, using his much greater size and the leverage of his standing position, pushed the gun down so that it was pointed at Wilson's left hip. Wilson, using his left arm as a brace, gained enough leverage to push the gun up level with the driver's door. Wilson then fired into the door, shattering the glass inside from the rolled down window.

Brown stepped back briefly, became 'enraged' and assaulted Wilson again with his [Brown's] head and arms again inside the cruiser. Wilson then fired another shot. Note that autopsy results and forensic analysis would later conform that these shots were fired from inside of Wilson's cruiser.

Brown then took off running. Wilson radioed for additional assistance, calling out that shots were fired. Wilson chased after Brown on foot, fearing that Brown's violently aggressive behavior was a danger to anyone he might next encounter.

Witness 104 was in a minivan stopped near Wilson's cruiser. According to her later testimony, after hearing the first two gunshots, she looked and saw that Brown's arms were inside the cruiser. She could not see what Brown and Wilson were doing because Brown's body blocked her view. Witness 104 saw Brown run from the cruiser, followed by Wilson, who ran after him while yelling "stop, stop, stop."

Wilson chased Brown, repeatedly yelling for Brown to stop and get on the ground. When Brown was about 20 to 30 feet from Wilson, he abruptly stopped and turned toward the officer. Wilson later stated that Brown looked "psychotic." Brown then 'grunted' and charged at Wilson, closing the distance between them to about 15 feet.

Wilson, fearing for his life, backed up as Brown ran toward him, repeatedly ordering Brown to stop and get on the ground. Brown kept charging at Wilson. Wilson later said that he knew if Brown reached him, he "would be done."

Witness 102 later described Brown as a "threat," moving at a "full charge." Witness 102 stated that Wilson only fired shots when Brown was running toward Wilson. It appeared to Witness 102 that Wilson's life was in jeopardy.

Witness 104 later described Brown's movement toward Wilson as a "tackle run," and stated that Brown "wasn't going to stop."

Wilson fired multiple shots and Brown paused. Wilson again yelled for Brown to get on the ground, and again Brown charged at him. Wilson backed up and fired again. Brown again very briefly paused, and Wilson again yelled for Brown to get on the ground. Brown once more lunged at Wilson as if he were going to "tackle" the Officer.

As Brown closed the distance between them to about eight to ten feet, Wilson fired again. The last shot fired entered Brown's head, and Brown "went down right there."

Witness 104 later explained that it took some time for Wilson to fire, adding that she "would have fired sooner."

Credible witness accounts and cellular phone video proved that Wilson did not touch Brown's body after Brown fell to the ground. Autopsy results later confirmed that Wilson did not shoot Brown in the back as Brown ran away. DNA analysis of Brown's blood on at various spots on the pavement established that Brown was moving toward Wilson as the shooting occurred.

Wilson immediately radioed, "Send me every car we got and a supervisor." Within seconds, additional officers arrived on the scene. Within minutes, local residents began "pouring onto the street." Some people in the growing crowd became hostile and there were voices stating "[We] need to kill these motherfuckers," referring to the officers on scene.

Witness 135 later explained to federal prosecutors that Brown's friend (Witness 101) ran away as soon as the first shot was fired and never returned. However, she described a young man matching Witness 101's description who later ran around the Canfield apartments while stating, "The police shot my friend and his hands were up." Witness 135 offered that this 'execution narrative' was quickly accepted and propagated by local residents. Witness 135 stated that is seemed these people used the 'execution narrative' as both an excuse to riot and to create a "block party" atmosphere.

Crime scene detectives were interrupted at least twice by what sounded like automatic gunfire in the area. They also had to deal with some local residents approaching the crime scene while calling out, "Kill the Police." Witnesses and officers described the scene as "volatile," and they were concerned for "both their personal safety and the integrity of the crime scene."

According to Witness 102, the crowds that gathered voiced the opinion that the police shot Brown for "no reason" and that he had his "hands up in surrender." Witness 102, who was at the scene, told another onlooker what had actually happened. Moments later, "two black women approached Witness 102, mobile phones set to record," and asked him to recount his statements. When Witness 102 declined to do so, the women responded with racial slurs, calling Witness 102 a "white motherfucker" (Witness 102 was actually biracial).

Witness 102 called 911 the following day to offer his report. On Monday, August 11, 2014, Witness 102 explained to police that he "felt bad about the situation," and he wanted to "bring closure to [Brown's] family," so no one would believe that the Officer Wilson "got away with murdering their son."

The physical evidence established that Wilson shot Brown once in the hand, at close range, while Wilson sat in his police cruiser, struggling with Brown for control of Wilson's gun. Wilson shot Brown several more times after Brown turned and confronted Wilson.

There was no credible evidence to refute Wilson's stated belief that he acted in self-defense. Wilson's account was thoroughly corroborated by all physical evidence, his own perception of the threat posed by Brown, and corroboration by several credible and consistent eyewitness accounts.

Investigators separated credible witnesses from those who were not. Much of the testimony from false witnesses was included in the Justice Report to demonstrate the difficulty of obtaining the true narrative.

For instance, Witness 125 "initially told law enforcement that she witnessed the shooting, but later recanted, claiming that she wanted to be involved from the outset and therefore lied to investigators." She testified that she hadn't actually witnessed any part of the incident and said she had initially done so "because she wanted to be part of something."

Witness 131 initially told the FBI that Wilson shot Brown only as Brown lunged forward. But he later told the county grand jury that Brown was standing still as he was shot to death and he denied that he said anything different to the FBI.

When Witness 112 was confronted with his own contradictory statements, he "became agitated and angry, and refused to listen to a recording of his previous statement." He could not explain the differences in his accounts or why his statements had changed.

During media interviews, Witness 118 claimed that she saw the "whole scenario play out." She told the media that "Wilson shot Brown in the back from three feet away and that Brown never moved back towards Wilson." When officials challenged the inconsistencies in her statements, Witness 118 admitted she had not witnessed the event and had assumed 'facts' based on discussions with other residents in the Canfield Green complex and by watching the news.

Witness 122 stated that Brown had turned around with his hands up and repeatedly screamed "Okay!" in surrender. Witness 122 also said that three officers were present during the shooting and that "the heavyset officer shot until he ran out of bullets." Officer Wilson had a slim build.

Witness 122 was unknowingly captured in a video taken minutes after the shooting. That video showed Witness 122 putting his hands up and saying, "He had his fucking hands in the air." Mr. Brown's family later stated that Witness 122 contacted them after the shooting and related that he had seen "Wilson shoot Brown execution-style as Brown was on his knees holding his hands in the air." When pressed by officials, Witness 122 denied making any such statements.

Witness 132 said that two police cruisers stopped Brown, the first of which ran over Brown's feet. Witness 132 said that Brown tried to run away but the officer shot Brown about five feet from the cruiser. After Brown fell to his knees and put his hands up, the "officer shot Brown eight or nine more times." After that interview with the FBI, Witness 132 "actively and successfully evaded service of a county grand jury subpoena." Witness 132 "ignored phone calls, hung up on the prosecutors, and pretended he was not at home."

Witness 126 said that she saw Brown on his knees with his hands up while Wilson advanced on Brown and shot him. After Brown fell face down to the ground, Wilson "finished him off." When the FBI told Witness 126 that her account was inconsistent with all evidence, she "became belligerent, grabbed the recording device, shut it off, and would not return it to the agents." Witness 126 then admitted that she had initially lied. When Witness 126 testified before the county grand jury, she denied being untruthful to the FBI and denied that she admitted to being untruthful to the FBI.

Witness 137 stated that after the police officer shot Brown in the back, Brown turned around with his hands up in surrender. The officer then fired "every round" into Brown, killing him "execution" style. Witness 137 said that after Brown fell forward, "the officer stood over him and finished him off." Witness 137 "referred to how clear the visual of events was to him." Witness 137 later admitted that he hadn't witnessed anything and had "assumed" that his version was true based on the sound of the bullets and "common sense."

Witness 128 initially stated that Brown said, "Don't kill me" before Wilson then fired two shots at "point blank range." These shots hit Brown in the face and Brown fell to the ground. Wilson then "fired four or five shots into Brown's back after Brown was already dead, face first on the ground." When pressed by federal prosecutors, Witness 128 said he might have "hallucinated" that scenario. He admitted that much of what he initially said was assumption.

Witness 128 spoke to Brown's mother on the day of the shooting and said that Wilson shot Brown at point blank range while Brown's hands were up. He added that, even after Brown fell to his death, "Wilson stood over Brown and fired several more times." Several individuals identified Witness 128 as one person who "was going around spreading a narrative that Brown was shot with his hands up in surrender" in the minutes and hours immediately after the event.

According to Witness 120, Wilson got out of his cruiser and advanced to within "a step away" from Brown. Witness 120 stated that he heard Brown say, "Please don't shoot me," just before Wilson shot Brown "point blank" in the head. Witness 120 later explained that while he did not actually see shooting, common sense dictated that "those eight shots struck Brown." He added that he based most of his prior statement on what people in the community were saying.

During their investigations, FBI agents and SLCPD detectives monitored social media, print media, and various television broadcasts and news reports in order to locate potential witnesses. Using these methods, they tracked down several people who claimed to have witnessed Brown's shooting. "All of these purported witnesses, upon being interviewed by law enforcement, acknowledged that they did not actually witness the shooting, but rather repeated what others told them in the immediate aftermath of the shooting."

SLCPD detectives conducted a more detailed interview with Officer Wilson on August 10, 2014. That night, a candlelight vigil to honor Brown turned violent. More than a dozen businesses were vandalized and looted. More than 30 people were arrested, and two police officers suffered injuries.

The FBI opened a federal criminal civil rights investigation on August 11, 2014. That day, Ferguson police and city leaders receive a number of death threats while hundreds gathered outside the Ferguson Police Department to demand justice for Brown's death.

On August 12, 2014, Rev. Al Sharpton arrived in St. Louis to speak to Brown's family and to "demand justice" in the fatal shooting.

That same day, President Obama stated, "We lost a young man, Michael Brown, in heartbreaking and tragic circumstances. He was 18 years old. His family will never hold Michael in their arms again," and "police should not be bullying or arresting journalists who are just trying to do their jobs and report to the American people on what they see on the ground." (2)

On August 13, 2014, the Obama Justice Department opened a federal civil rights investigation related to the Ferguson shooting.

On September 28, 2014, President Obama spoke at the Congressional Black Congress's awards dinner. He stated, "I won't comment on the [ongoing] investigation. I know that Michael's family is here tonight. I know that nothing any of us can say can ease the grief of losing a child so soon. But the anger and the emotion that followed his death awakened our nation once again to the reality that people in this room have long understood, which is, in too many communities around the country, a gulf of mistrust exists between local residents and law enforcement." (3)

Obama continued, "Too many young men of color feel targeted by law enforcement, guilty of walking while black, or driving while black, judged by stereotypes that fuel fear and resentment and hopelessness."

In 2017, a settlement was reached in the Brown family's wrongful death lawsuit against the city.

DISCUSSION:

The false narrative around Michael Brown began in Mr. Brown's community almost immediately after his death. Faulty assumptions and outright lies spread quickly and were amplified by the national media and the President himself.

There was no evidence to suggest that Brown's death was racially motivated. All evidence shows that he was justifiably killed after violently assaulting a police officer and then threatening to do so again.

Obama's public statements and overt support of Mr. Brown could have only suggested to the public that Brown's death was the result of racial targeting by law enforcement, which in turn could only further fuel fear and resentment.

Obama's explicit support for the false narrative being woven around Michael Brown's death served to further divide the country and worsen race relations. Note that Officer Wilson, even when fully exonerated, was never invited to any Presidential events or mentioned by President Obama.

As of this writing Brown's image still appears on the official BLM website and he is specifically mentioned as a martyr for the BLM cause. No credible evidence supports this.

CHAPTER SIX.
TAMIR RICE.

On Nov. 22, 2014, Tamir Rice was at the Cudell Park Recreation Center (CPRC) in Cleveland, Ohio. Tamir was seen holding a toy black airsoft pistol with a removable magazine that was "virtually indistinguishable" (according to the US Justice Report dated 12.29.2020) (1) from a real .45 Colt semi-automatic pistol. Tamir periodically pointed the gun at individuals at the CPRC and at the adjoining playground.

At approximately 3:11 p.m., an individual made a "911" call to report that a "guy with a pistol" was pointing a gun at several people on the playground at the CPRC. The caller described the scene as very frightening. The caller added that the suspected person might be a juvenile and that the gun might be a fake. On the date of the incident, Tamir was 12-years-old and stood 5'7" and 195 lbs.

A 911 dispatcher broadcast the call as a "Code 1" (the highest priority call) and Officers Garmback and Loehmann radioed that they would respond. The dispatcher relayed to Officers Garmback and Loehmann that "there's a black male sitting on the swing. He's wearing a camouflage hat, a gray jacket with black sleeves. He keeps pulling a gun out of his pants and pointing it at people."

The dispatcher did not relay that the individual might be a juvenile or that the gun might be fake. Thus, the officers believed that they were responding to a scene where an adult male was leveling a real gun at several individuals, presumably including children.

Video from a nearby surveillance camera captured the subsequent events. Investigators noted that the video footage was grainy, shot from a distance, did not show detail or perspective, and that portions of the incident were not visible because of the location of the patrol car. Also, the camera's time-lapse function captured only two frames per second. This was insufficient to record continuous action.

As the Officers approached the CPRC's playground area with a swing set, Tamir was sitting alone at a picnic table in a gazebo. He matched the description provided by the dispatcher. No one else was in the immediate area.

In the video, Tamir stood up from the picnic table approximately 10 seconds before the shooting. In those first three seconds, Tamir walked around the end of the table and continued toward the general direction of the oncoming patrol car.

Officer Garmback attempted to stop the patrol car, but it slid forward on the wet ground, ultimately stopping a very short distance from Tamir. Officer Loehmann exited the still moving patrol car. At that moment, it Tamir made movements with both his left and right arms around his waistband. Officer Loehmann fired two shots within less than two seconds of opening the passenger door, striking Tamir once in the abdomen.

Meanwhile, Officer Garmback exited the patrol car and began moving to the front of the vehicle, where he stood for approximately 15 seconds with his gun drawn and pointing in Tamir's direction. Enhanced video showed a dark object (the gun) on the floor of the gazebo within a few feet of Tamir. Officer Garmback then moved into the gazebo and kicked the toy gun and magazine further away from Tamir.

After Officer Garmback kicked the gun and magazine into the grass, he reported the shots fired and requested emergency medical assistance.

On December 4, 2014, US Attorney General Eric Holder addressed the findings of an investigation into the Cleveland Division of Police. He stated, "In recent days, millions of people throughout the nation have come together – bound by grief and anguish – in response to the tragic deaths of Michael Brown, in Ferguson, Missouri, and Eric Garner, in New York City." (2)

On December 29, 2020, The US Justice Department announced that the prosecutors reviewing the independent federal investigation into the fatal shooting of Tamir Rice found insufficient evidence to support federal criminal charges against Cleveland Division of Police. (1)

DISCUSSION.

There was no evidence to suggest that Tamir Rice's death was racially motivated. All evidence shows that he was killed as a result of tragic circumstances and the unfortunate choice to aim a realistic toy gun at strangers in public.

CHAPTER SEVEN.
BREONNA TAYLOR.

Few cases in the past several years have gained as much attention as Breonna Taylor's.

Here are the facts. (1)

On December 3, 2016, the Louisville Metropolitan Police Department (LMPD) discovered their most recent homicide victim in a rental car. The car was registered to Breonna Taylor. Ms. Taylor's address was 3003 Springfield Drive, Apartment Number 4, Louisville, KY, 40214. When police arrived at that address to question Ms. Taylor, they also found Mr. Jamarcus Glover in the apartment. The homicide victim, Fernandez Bowan, was the brother of Demarius Bowman, an associate of Jamarcus Glover. Demarius Bowman and Jamarcus Glover had been arrested together "numerous times."

During that interview with police, Ms. Taylor stated that she did not know the victim and only found out what happened from Mr. Glover. Ms. Taylor stated that she and Mr. Glover has been dating for "3-4 months" and that she allowed him to drive her rental car.

Ms. Taylor posted bond for Mr. Glover when he was arrested on an unrelated felony charge on March 9, 2016, and again for a misdemeanor arrest on January 4, 2017.

In December 2019, LMPD suspected that the residences at 2424 Elliott Avenue and 2605 West Muhammad Ali Boulevard, Louisville Kentucky, 40211, were involved in drug trafficking. This suspicion was based on "calls for service" in that neighborhood and "narcotics related crime tips" received.

Note that Ms. Taylor also posted a $2,500 bond for a Darreal Forrest on December 31, 2019. Mr. Forrest's residence was listed as 2605 West Muhammad Ali Boulevard in Louisville. He had been arrested for "Convicted Felon in Possession of a Firearm," "TICS [Trafficking in Controlled Substance] 1ST DEGREE, 1ST OFFENSE (>=4GMS COCAINE)" "DRUG PARAPHENALIA – BUY/POSSESS" and "TRAFFIC IN MARIJUANA, LESS THAN 8 OZ – 1ST OFFENSE."

On January 2, 2020, LMPD set up a surveillance camera and began watching the house at

2424 Elliott Avenue. "Within an hour of the pole camera being installed, PBI [Place Based Investigation] detectives witnessed 15-20 vehicles go to and from 2424 Elliott Avenue for a short period of time which is indicative of narcotics trafficking." That evening, PBI saw a white 2016 Chevy Impala drop off Jamarcus Glover at 2424 Elliott Avenue. That car was registered to Breonna Taylor at her 3003 Springfield Drive address.

Later still on January 2, 2020, LMPD executed search warrants at 2424 Elliott Avenue and 2605 West Muhammad Ali Boulevard. They arrested Jamarcus Glover on an outstanding warrant. The search done by police at these two addresses discovered crack cocaine, marijuana, a stolen handgun and assorted drug paraphernalia.

On January 3, 2020, Mr. Glover called Ms. Taylor from jail. These calls were recorded. Mr. Glover asked Ms. Taylor to call [name redacted from transcript] and tells her this person has "got my fucking money."

During a separate phone call with Mr. Glover that day, Ms. Taylor said that she had spoken to [name redacted from transcript] and that this person was "already back at the trap." Note that a "trap" or "trap house" is a common term for a drug house used to sell drugs, synthesize drugs or shelter drug users consuming drugs.

Ms. Taylor then said that "they couldn't post bond [for Mr. Glover] till one."

To this, Mr. Glover replied, "Just be on standby so you can come get me...Love you."

Ms. Taylor answered, "Love you too."

Ms. Taylor's phone received 48 separate calls from jail inmates from January 1, 2020 to January 3, 2020, including 26 calls from Mr. Glover after his January 2, 2020 arrest.

On January 9, 2020, PBI detectives asked for a warrant to install a tracking device on a red 2017 Dodge Charger they believed was involved in drug trafficking. Between January 12, 2020, and January 30, 2020, this vehicle went to Ms. Taylor's 3003 Springfield Drive address six times. One of these visits occurred on January 16, 2020, when PBI detectives photographed Jamarcus Glover exit the tracked Dodge Charger, briefly enter Ms. Taylor's apartment and exit with a "USPS package in his right hand." Mr. Glover then got back into the tracked Dodge Charger and drove directly to 2605 West Muhammad Ali Boulevard.

On February 13, 2020, PBI detectives recorded a black Dodge Charger pull up outside of 2424 Elliott Avenue. This Dodge Charger was registered to Ms. Taylor at her 3003 Springfield Drive address. Jamarcus Glover exited the driver's seat and entered 2424 Elliott Avenue. Three minutes later, PBI detectives "observed Breonna Taylor get out of the passenger side of the vehicle and look around for a few seconds before she got back into the vehicle." Five minutes after he entered 2424 Elliott Avenue, Mr. Glover exited that house and reentered Ms. Taylor's car before it was driven away.

The report added, "It is important to note that PBI detectives have observed on the pole camera Breonna Taylor's black Dodge Charger (KY [license plate number redacted]) pull up in front of 2424

Elliott Avenue numerous times at varying hours of the day/night."

On February 14, 2020, LMPD towed the red 2017 Dodge Charger from 2605 West Muhammad Ali Boulevard for a parking violation. Jamarcus Glover then went to the police station to file a complaint against the officer who had the car towed. Mr. Glover "gave the phone number [number redacted] to contact him which is registered to Breonna Taylor."

Note that, as of February 20, 2020, Mr. Glover was listing Ms. Taylor's 3003 Springfield Drive address as his residential address. On February 24, 2020, PBI detectives obtained Jamarcus Glover's Chase Bank records. These bank statements also listed Ms. Taylor's 3003 Springfield Drive address as Mr. Glover's residence.

A search warrant was requested on March 12, 2020. The one item in clear and valid contention was the statement which bagin, "9.) Affiant verified through a US Postal Inspector that Jamarcus Glover has been receiving packages at 3003 Springfield Drive #4" No Postal Inspector supported that claim during the subsequent investigation.

The end of article nine of the Breonna Taylor warrant reads, "Affiant believes through training and experience, that Mr. J Glover may be keeping narcotics and/or proceeds from the sale of narcotics at 3003 Springfield Drive #4 for safe keeping." This seems entirely accurate. Mr. Glover would apparently (if unintentionally) confirm this himself from jail on March 13, 2020.

On March 13, 2020, PBI detectives, CDI (Criminal Interdiction Division) detectives and SWAT

Team officers executed simultaneous search warrants at 2424 Elliott Avenue and 3003 Springfield Drive Apartment Number 4 (as well as two other addresses). Jamarcus Glover was arrested at 2424 Elliott Avenue and officers found crack cocaine, fentanyl, "a large amount of US currency digital scales, and other evidence of narcotics trafficking within the residence," as well as evidence of "attempts to destroy suspected cocaine by placing it inside the toilet tank in the residence."

The paperwork provided on the LMPD's official web page dedicated to the shooting of Breonna Taylor stated that she was "the main target on a narcotics search warrant for 3003 Springfield Drive #4." The actual warrant suggests she was one of three main targets at that address, the other two being Jamarcus Glover and Adrian Walker.

Breonna Taylor was tragically killed as the officers served the warrant early on March 13, 2020.

Later on March 13, 2020, Jamarcus Glover had a telephone conversation from jail with a female whose name was redacted from the call's transcript. This female asked Mr. Glover, "So where your money at?"

Mr. Glover answered, "Where my money at? Bre [Breonna Taylor] had like $8 grand."

The female asked, "Bre had $8 grand of your money?"

Mr. Glover answered, "Yeah."

At that point, another unknown male joined the call. Mr. Glover said to him that Breonna Taylor had "the $8 grand I gave her the other day and she picked up another $6 (grand)."

Mr. Glover later stated, "Bre been handling all my money, she been handling my money...She been handling shit for me and cuz, it ain't just me."

Still later in the conversation, the female participant in the call said to Mr. Glover, "Motherfuckers are posting videos of you and all that."

Mr. Glover asked, "Who posts videos of me?"

The female answered, "This bitch (Bre) where she'd been with you, since you ain't been over at my house... the same day you post a picture I guess she post a video, you knew it because she said what's up she was in the bed with you, you kissing all over her. This shit is embarrassing."

Still later in the day, Jamarcus Glover had another telephone conversation with an unknown male. Mr. Glover told this person, "Bre got that charger [possibly referring to the Dodge Charger] and all that shit... Bre's paper trail makes sense for everything she got though."

Later in this call, the unknown male stated, "Then on top of that they [the police] go over there [to Breonna Taylor's apartment] and find money."

Mr. Glover stated, "They didn't find nothing in her house."

The unknown male asked, "I thought you said they found some money over there?"

Mr. Glover said, "It was there... They [the police] didn't do nothing though."

The unknown male asked, "So they didn't take none of the money?"

Mr. Glover answered, "Kenneth said that none of that go on. He said Homicide came straight on the scene and they went to packing Bre and they left."

On March 25, 2020, Officer Jon Mattingly was interviewed. In the transcript he was asked by the interviewer, "Now, what kind of information if – if anything at all were you guys given in the preoperational brief?"

Officer Mattingly answered, "She [Breonna Taylor] held – possibly held dope for him [Jamarcus Glover]. Received packages and held his money."

Mattingly added during this interview that they believed Breonna Taylor would be alone in her apartment because they knew Jamarcus Glover had already been arrested at the 2424 Elliott Avenue address and that Breonna Taylor was the sole target of the warrant executed at her 3003 Springfield Drive, Apartment Number 4 address. He added that, while the warrant was written as a "no knock" warrant the involved officers opted for a "knock and announce" technique.

An interview was conducted with the civilian witness to the warrant executed at Breonna Taylor's 3003 Springfield Drive, Apartment Number 4 address. This interview has both its date and the civilian witness's name redacted.

The interviewer asked, "Okay, did you hear them saying anything as they were knocking?"

The witness responded, "Oh, "This is the cops.""

"This is the cops," said the interviewer.

"Yeah," said the witness.

Later, the interviewer asked, "When you opened up the door [to your apartment] you could hear them [the police] saying this is the cops and you heard them knocking on the door?"

"Yeah," answered the witness.

All of these details are available to the public. (1) Reviewing them is uncomfortable and discussing them is perhaps dangerous. But to allow false narratives to increase divisiveness and drive public policy is irresponsible.

On May 20, 2020, the official BLM global Network website aired their video, "Say Her Name – Breonna Taylor, a Conversation with Tamika Mallory and Taylor Family Attorney Lonita Baker." (2)

Kailee Scales, still the Managing Director of BLM, stated (at the 1:00 minute mark) that "This case is, um, traumatizing all of us. It's, it's horrible... We hear about our sister Breonna with her beautiful, loving smile and we hear the story and we're sucker-punched again... We need justice for Breonna. We have to, um, just do the thing."

Lonita Baker stated (at the 4:31 mark), "We filed suit in the middle of April, a civil suit against the three officers involved."

Sadly, it would be surprising if a civil suit *wasn't* quickly filed after such an incident. But at the time that suit was filed and even in mid-May when this video was released, investigations were ongoing and there was no comprehensive understand of what lead to Ms. Taylor's death. This conversation, lead by

BLM's Kailee Scales, was based on limited insight and assumptions. The primary assumption, of course, was that Ms. Taylor's death was racially motivated. This assumption was spoken of as truth, despite there being no evidence of any kind to support it.

In this case, as in so many others, BLM immediately assumed the involved officers acted upon racial prejudice rather than upon the hard evidence they had gathered. BLM kept race as the only lens through which to see this tragic case. The uncomfortable facts regarding Ms. Taylor's long-running and very close relationship with felonious drug dealers, the very facts that gave LMPD a valid cause to arrive on her doorstep, are never addressed.

Ms. Scales goes on to ask (at 11:29), "So, so what happens next, Tamika? What do we do next? Because this is obviously, this is obviously a part of a big, systemic issue to dehumanize us. To criminalize us. Um, to make us afraid. To, ah, to strip us of our dignity and our freedom. Um, what happens now?"

Here Ms. Scales leans into Critical Theory by stating that this death was "obviously" part of a "systemic issue." As we've seen before and will see repeatedly in the pages that follow, BLM leaders across the US assume that every negative interaction between police and Black people is automatically and completely racist. They never offer supporting evidence and often makes such claims in spite of overwhelming evidence to the contrary.

When speaking of her set of 'demands,' Lonita Baker stated (22:22) "That the officers be fired. And two, that they be prosecuted to the full extent of the law. And here recently we are calling on the Chief of Police to resign." She added (22:58), "And Mayor

Fischer, if you're not going to force, if he [the Chief of Police] doesn't resign and you're not gonna fire him, then Mayor maybe it's time for you to go too."

"Right," Ms. Scales responded. "Yeah."

This is 'justice' as defined by current Social Justice crusaders. They assume that Critical Theory dominance-submission power hierarchies permeate every social interaction. They then assume, with no evidence, that these interactions are inherently racist. Next, they assume the White participant's guilt, ignoring actual evidence that contradicts their assumptions and each person's right to due process.

This constant, hollow drumbeat of racial victimization fuels everything from massive, violent, days-long protests as well as subtler yet sinister incidents like the one that played out in Smith College in 2018 (3). It also shreds the credibility of Social Justice activists while fatiguing society's empathy for such cases. This harms those People of Color who are truly hurt by racially biased police.

Ms. Baker actually hit upon the most salient point when she added (29:10), "We have to ban the practice of no-knock warrants. Because it's killing too many innocent people." No-knock warrants allow police to enter unannounced, preventing suspects from destroying evidence. But there a thousand ways they can go wrong.

During a protest in Louisville on May 26, 2020, that included Breonna Taylor's friends and family, demonstrators stood outside Mayor Greg Fischer's house and demanded the arrest of the officers involved in her killing. This demand was amplified online and included a Change.org petition calling for

examples Mr. Giger gives here are clearly not murder (unless one opts to disregard facts and evidence and live in a disgruntled personal fantasy).

In December 2019, when an Officer involved in Mr. Anderson's case was promoted, Jorden Giger was quoted as saying, "This is why people in the black community have issues with police, because of these kinds of things." (5) The Officer was promoted by South Bend's Board of Public Safety, which at that time was predominantly Black.

As in so many other instances, this reflexive and almost complete negation of truth in favor of an Identity Politics agenda further erodes any credibility these people might claim. The four speakers in this video are educated people and savvy enough to participate in the highly organized and well-funded BLM Global Network. They had access to all of these facts. They either intentionally presented a false narrative (perhaps in the hope that their viewers were too trusting or too lazy to fact check) or they were so fully 'woke,' so fully devote to their Critical Theory orthodoxy, that they actually believed in this narrative. The latter scenario is much more frightening.

Mr. Giger then added (10:34) "We knew that this [the Eric Logan case] was gonna, wa-, that this was gonna take off like wildfire. And when you have those moments, um, where, uh, Black folks are paying attention and they're demanding justice you gotta be there. You've gotta be there. You've gotta show up to provide direction." And so, (11:37) "We had a series of protests. We, we disrupted uh, uh, uh, a national press conference that Pete Buttigieg was having, uh, um, at a local high school here."

Jordan Giger later stated (26:47) "So we thought, okay, this is great. Right? Like we, we protested, we held disruptions. Right? We had a twenty-four hour, um, uh, essentially standoff outside of the County-City Building." Later he stated (34:14) "Yeah, we disrupt. But, you know, when disrupt we come with facts. I mean we are, you know we have substance to us. We're not just screaming and yelling."

The modus operandi Mr. Giger seems to promote here is an opportunistic method of disrupting and demanding. These speakers don't offer viable solutions. They demand. They do this while ignoring facts at the expense of any "substance" they might have.

Emmanuel Cannady stated (16:53) "Because we, we, we, we don't really espouse to this bad apple sort of idea. There's a bad cop here, bad cop here. But it's a culture that complicit in allowing these bad apples to really, um, uh, do their, their, their dirty work that, that they're doing. So we wanna address, yes, we wanna get bad officers out there but we also wanna address the culture. Hence why we wanted to get what is the whole department looking at in terms of cultural competency."

Ms. Redding added a similar sentiment when she said (41:39) "This is the time for accountability. You have to have accountable at your house. You have to have accountability in your community. And you definitely have to have, hold these leaders accountable."

Personal accountability and insightful, self-critical cultural awareness are noble aims and qualities. It would be interesting to discuss with these our BLM representatives the ways in which Eric Logan and Michael Anderson exhibited these aims and qualities. Were these two men "bad apples" in a well-intentioned but flawed culture? Did they display accountability and did their culture hold them accountable? (Of course, every culture has its flaws and hopefully all are well-intentioned. Modern Social Justice culture, with its increasing venom and vitriol and its hatefully intolerant Identity Politics and rotten Critical Theory festering in its core is a likely exception.)

Mr. Cannady aligned himself with the agenda-driven Identity Politics of the Black Lives Matter Global Network and was complicit in the skewed and falsified narrative woven around Eric Logan. He cannot pretend to purely and impartially "research" anything. In March 2020, Mr. Cannady exposed his anti-White bias when he publicly reacted to a news conference regarding Eric Logan. Special Prosecutor Ric Hertel announced that Mr. Logan's death was the result of justified police action. Mr. Cannady called these findings, "a farce, a sham," and "The only thing I learned from this is there's no justice for black men." (6)

Ms. Redding and Mr. Giger comment during the video about how they caused Pete Buttigieg's downfall. Of course, through some back room dealings, Mayor Pete went on to land a Cabinet post in the Biden administration. BLM's silence about this has been deafening.

DISCUSSION.

There was no evidence to suggest that the deaths of Eric Logan or Michael Anderson were racially motivated. All evidence shows that they died as a direct result of their own actions (assaulting an officer with a deadly weapon and attempting to swallow baggies of drugs while sprinting from police, respectively).

CHAPTER NINE.
THE FALSE NARRATIVES OF BLM LOS ANGELES.

CHRISTOPHER DEANDRE MITCHELL. BLM LA.

The Black Lives Matter Los Angeles chapter posted the following:

"Police associations have long declared war on the people...with targets on the backs of Black people, in particular. Their members routinely perpetrate acts of state violence... Police associations function as organized crime... It's time that their reign of terror be brought to an end."

It continued, "Christopher Deandre Mitchell was killed on December 9, 2018 by Torrance police officers Anthony Chavez and Matthew Concannon. The two officers still haven't been fired."

The *Officer Involved Shooting of Christopher Deandre Mitchell Torrance Police Department* authorized by Jackie Lacey, LA's District Attorney, was dated October 9, 2019. (1)

Mitchell was found in the driver's seat of a stolen car. Officers were about to detain for suspected grand theft auto. As the officers approached, they observed what appeared to be a gun in Mitchell's lap. Mitchell moved his hands toward the weapon.

Mitchell was given repeated commands to raise his hands and exit the car. Mitchell complied with none of these instructions and instead lowered his hands toward what the officers believed was a deadly weapon. "Reasonably fearing for his and his partner's lives, Concannon fired an initial shot from his service weapon. An instant later, Chavez fired twice from the other side of the car."

The BLM Los Angeles Chapter reacted to this decision by posting, "She [Jackie Lacey] officially issued her decision not to prosecute the Torrance police officers who murdered #ChristopherDeAndreMitchell on December 9, 2018 within 15 seconds of approaching his vehicle."

"As is her practice, she participated in the secondary murder of Christopher — the assassination of his character — regurgitating the police account, which claimed that he was "armed" with a toy gun."

"Since the time of his murder, we have been standing with the family demanding the release of the names of the officers."

DISCUSSION.

There was no evidence to suggest that Christopher Michael's death was racially motivated. All evidence shows that he was killed by police while reaching for a gun while seated in a stolen car.

BOYCOTT 24 HOUR FITNESS. ALBERT DORSEY and DENNIS TODD ROGERS, BLM LOS ANGELES.

As of March 24, 2021, BLM Las Angeles was calling for a state-wide protest of all 24 Hour Fitness locations.

They stated:

"If the staff of 24 Hour Fitness didn't call the police when having issues with Black people in their facilities, <u>Dennis Todd Rogers</u> and <u>Albert Ramon Dorsey</u> would be alive.

In the wake of the two deaths, Black Lives Matter Los Angeles made a set of demands:

- Issue and widely disseminate a public statement affirming the value of Black lives;

- Immediately establish and conduct a series of mandatory and substantial cultural-competency training sessions for managers, workers, and franchisees;

- Develop protocols and alternatives to calling the police and make sure all staff understand and accept the procedures.

After the company ignored these demands, Black Lives Matter Los Angeles began weekly protests outside of disparate 24 Hour Fitness locations around California, starting January 31st, 2019, the day Albert Ramon Dorsey would have turned 32 years old.

We have gotten petitions supporting our demands signed by members, protesting the

128

company's lack of response to its responsibility in these two deaths.

We have gotten more than 100 people to cancel their memberships to 24 Hour Fitness.

We even took a group of protesters to the San Ramon corporate headquarters to deliver these petitions and demands, only to be rebuffed by company representatives.

When will 24 Hour Fitness follow at least the <u>basic standard of corporate responsibility Starbucks showed</u> as a sign of contrition?" (2)

The official *Officer Involved Shooting of Albert Dorsey Los Angeles Police Department* report (3) was authorized by Jackie Lacey, District Attorney. This was released on July 28, 2020.

On October 22, 2018, Albert Dorsey purchased a membership at the 24-Hour Fitness located in Hollywood. On October 28, 2018, at approximately 4:30 a.m., Dorsey was walking around outside the 24-Hour Fitness location yelling. When a security guard approached and asked to leave, Dorsey repeatedly punched the guard in the face. This knocked the security guard unconscious, and he was hospitalized for several days. LAPD responded to the incident, but Dorsey had already left the scene. A battery report was taken.

On October 29, 2020, Dorsey returned to this 24 Hour Fitness location. When he passed by the front counter Luis C. told him he needed to "punch- in." Dorsey replied, "If I'm going to punch anybody, it's going to be you" and continued walking into the facility.

The 24 Hour Fitness employees then called police (the first of their three 9-11 calls about Mr. Dorsey in about 30 minutes) and reported that Mr. Dorsey was acting in a "threatening manner and refusing to leave."

Prior to the officers arriving, Dorsey had several negative interactions with other patrons who tried to use the locker room, including one where he threatened to "fuck up" another member. A security guard asked Mr. Dorsey to leave. Mr. Dorsey refused.

When police arrived, they repeatedly instructed Mr. Dorsey to leave. Mr. Dorsey, "mostly ignored the officers while they encouraged him to hurry up and put on his clothes. At one point, Dorsey began dancing and [Officer] Rodriguez told him, "Hurry up! Stop dancing! Hurry up!" Dorsey responded by calling Rodriguez a "bitch," continuing to dance, and extending his middle finger at the officers."

After Mr. Dorsey repeatedly refused to leave the building, Officer Agdeppa produced a pair of handcuffs and he and Officer Rodriguez approached Dorsey. Mr. Dorsey resisted arrest and "pulled his handcuffed right arm away from Rodriguez's grasp and elbowed her in the face."

This caused Officer Agdeppa to draw his tazer and deploy it. However, the tase only seemed to further agitate Dorsey and he [Dorsey] began to throw punches at Rodriguez. Rodriguez activated her Taser for a second and third time, which had no apparent effect on Dorsey. Dorsey then struck Rodriguez with his right hand while grabbing for her Taser with his eft. Agdeppa then used his Taser in drive-stun mode or a second time. This caused Dorsey to turn on Agdeppa and "punch him in the face multiple times."

When Officer Agdeppa stumbled away, Dorsey urned on Rodriguez and punched her in the face hree to four times. He then pushed her, and she fell o the floor on her back. Mr. Dorsey then straddled Officer Rodriguez and began punching her again.

When Agdeppa again approached, Dorsey grabbed Agdeppa's holstered gun. Dorsey was unable o get the gun and Agdeppa pushed Dorsey away from him and said, "Don't make me do this! Stop!" Dorsey eplied by saying, "What the fuck are you going to do?" and "You ain't doing shit to me!"

Dorsey then grabbed [24 Hour Fitness employee] Luis C. by the jacket, pushed him, and then grabbed [security guard] Miguel C. by the neck with one hand and began choking him." When Miguel C. freed himself from the chokehold, Mr. Dorsey then reached for Agdeppa again and Agdeppa pushed Dorsey away and began shooting. Miguel C. believes Agdeppa fired five rounds and Dorsey fell to the ground and landed under a sink."

DISCUSSION.

There was no evidence to suggest that Albert Dorsey's death was racially motivated. All evidence shows that he was killed while violently and repeatedly assaulting both police officers and employees of 24 Fitness.

The *Officer Involved Shooting of Dennis Todd Williams-Rogers Los Angeles County Sheriff's Department* report (4) was authorized by District Attorney Jackie Lacey and dated February 21, 2018.

On March 7, 2017, sheriff's deputies responded to a disturbance call at a 24 Hour Fitness club on West Slauson Avenue. The club's manager (identified here as Julius N.) stated that Mr. Dennis Todd (Williams) Rogers was bothering other patrons. The officers "peacefully escorted Rogers" outside where the club's manager told Mr. Roger his membership was suspended for 24 hours. The officers left the scene.

However, Mr. Rogers remained outside the club. When he saw the manager preparing to exit, Mr. Rogers reached into his backpack and yelled to Julius N., "Come outside! I'm going to get you! I'm going to get you! I've been waiting on you!" Julius N. was frightened, believed Rogers may be reaching for a weapon and was too scared to walk to his car by himself. The armed security officer at the location, Jackey G., feared a possible armed confrontation. Julius N. called the Sheriff's Department and requested further assistance.

Deputies returned to this club and noticed Rogers appeared to be agitated. One deputy spoke with Mr. Rogers, who stated that when either Julius N. or Jackey G. exited the building, he was "going to fuck them up!" Seeing Rogers was irate and believing he was possibly unstable, Deputy Garcia requested a supervisor respond to their location.

Rogers remained outside the club, pacing back and forth with his backpack and calling the deputies "fake cops." Mr. Rogers continued to harass patrons as they entered and exited the gym. At one point, Mr. Rogers approached Deputy Imaizumi and threatened to kill him. When Mr. Rogers saw Julius N. standing inside the club's glass front doors, he approached the doors and yelled, "I'm gonna fuck you up!"

When Deputy Garcia approached the club to speak with Julius N., Mr. Rogers attempted to follow. When Deputy Garcia told Mr. Rogers to stay back, Mr. Rogers aggressively approached the officer and responded, "You want to fight! I'll fuck you up too!" Deputy Imaizumi saw Mr. Rogers' hostile and threatening behavior toward his partner. He yelled "Taser! Taser! Taser!" and deployed his Taser at Rogers. The Taser did not appear to affect Rogers, who ripped one or both Taser wires from his body.

Mr. Rogers then walked into an adjacent parking lot as four responding sheriff's deputies followed him at a distance.

Mr. Rogers paused, placed his backpack on the ground and reached into the bag. Believing he was retrieving a weapon, the deputies yelled, "Let me see your hands!" Rogers removed an electric hair clippers from a box inside his backpack and yelled, "I'm gonna fuck you guys up! I'm gonna kill one of you!" Deputy Imaizumi drew his weapon and radioed for emergency assistance.

Mr. Rogers swung the clippers "lasso-type technique" via the attached the cord and advanced upon Deputy Garcia. Garcia "was unable to determine what the object Rogers swung was, but did believe the object had a shiny blade attached." Rogers swung the object to within inches of Garcia's head, at eye level. Garcia yelled "Taser!" and deployed his Taser at

Rogers. Again the Taser had no obvious effect on Mr. Rogers, who again removed the prongs from his body.

Mr. Rogers then turned upon Deputy Imaizumi, saying, "I'm gonna fuck you up! I'm gonna kill you!" Imaizumi said Rogers charged at him several times while swinging the hair clippers. Imaizumi saw the hair clippers had a sharp edge and backed away from Rogers to avoid being struck. Imaizumi believed the hair clippers could have knocked him out, or cut his eyes or throat had the clippers stuck him.

Mr. Rogers aggressively charged at Imaizumi, suddenly closing the distance between them rapidly. Imaizumi back pedaled, pulled his duty weapon back to his hip to avoid being struck by the hair clippers, and raised his left hand to protect his face and neck. In fear of being seriously injured by Rogers, he fired his weapon. Rogers fell to the ground with his hands under his body.

Imaizumi immediately broadcast the officer involved shooting. Paramedics arrived at the scene, treated Mr. Rogers and transported him to Ronald Reagan UCLA Medical Center. At the hospital, "Despite life saving measures, Rogers succumbed to his injuries."

DISCUSSION.

There was no evidence to suggest that Dennis Todd Rogers death was racially motivated. All evidence shows that he was killed while violently assaulting police officers.

The Black Lives Matter Los Angeles chapter, it appears, has been hijacked by people so emotionally engaged in activism that they have entirely abandoned rational thought. These three tragic events (the first had video evidence, the last two had credible civilian witnesses) do not support BLM Los Angeles when they cry out about police and their 'war on the people,' their 'targets on the backs of Black people,' their 'acts of state violence' or any 'function as organized crime.'

The BLM leaders purposefully, repeatedly and very publicly villainize the brave law enforcement offers who responded to these dangerous scenes. This should insult and outrage every thinking person who values truth, reason and any pure sense of justice (a word coopted for vile purposes too often by these self-righteous and blatantly wrong activists).

CHAPTER TEN.
THE FALSE NARRATIVE OF BLM CHICAGO.

The homepage for the Chicago chapter of Black Lives Matter has a link titled 'Justice for Families.' (1) The Justice for Families page highlights dozens of Black individuals who died during interactions with police over the last several years.

This page states, "We honor your lives. We speak your names. We refuse to allow you to be erased."

BLM Chicago does not define 'justice' or give any indication of what that would entail. One has to assume that each individual case involved some 'injustice' that needs remedy. Simply scrolling down the page and looking through the names and faces of those who died at the hands of Chicago's police gives one the sense of some massive injustice.

But was there an affront to justice in each of these cases?

Investigating the tragic details reveals that, sadly, most of these deaths were the result of the decedents' poor choices and the justified action of police. Investigating these painful details disproves the 'injustice' narrative offered by BLM Chicago, which is the stated purpose of this book. This effort does not in any way seek to diminish the humanity and inherent value of those whose lives were lost. That stated, it is an insult to the brave police officers involved to allow such false narratives to persist.

CLEOTHA MITCHELL. (2)

On November 25, 2016, Cleotha Mitchell was shot and killed by a Chicago Police Officer after Mr. Mitchell fired a gun outside of Sky Box Bar, killing Jeffrey Banks and injuring Jerry Buckner.

Jeffrey Banks and Cleotha Mitchell went outside of the bar and entered into a verbal argument. The two men began to push each other. Jerry Buckner and others attempted to break up the fight when Mitchell produced a gun and fired a gun several times. The gunfire struck Buckner in the left arm. Banks ran away and Mitchell pursued him.

Officers in the immediate area heard these gunshots and converged on the scene. As these officers arrived, they witnessed Mr. Mitchell murder Mr. Banks. Mitchell fired his gun twice, striking Banks who fell to the ground dead. The officers ordered Mitchell to drop his gun, but Mitchell ignored the verbal commands. Officer Page fired his gun four times at Mitchell, fatally wounding him.

BLM Chicago does not mention justice for Mr. Banks or Mr. Buckner.

DISCUSSION.

There was no evidence to suggest that Cleotha Mitchell's death was racially motivated. All evidence shows that he was killed by police while actively committing homicide.

JOSHUA BEAL. (3)

On November 5, 2016, Joshua Beal and a group of his family and friends departed a funeral on the south side of Chicago. As their cars were caravanned down the street, the group exited their cars and blocked access to a fire station. After observing this, an off-duty Chicago Firefighter exited his vehicle and instructed the group to continue moving in order to clear the access to the firehouse.

The group of mourners physically confronted with the off-duty firefighter and began beating him. Two off-duty Chicago Police Officers (one who was in uniform) were driving by and stopped to break up the altercation. Both officers identified themselves as police officers and both officers drew their weapons. Joshua Beal pulled a handgun from his vehicle and pointed it at one Officer and other civilians. Beal attempted to fire the weapon, but the gun malfunctioned, causing a cartridge to get jammed in the ejection port.

Both of these officers fired several times striking Beal. Beal's gun was recovered near his body in a slide-lock position, which occurs when the slide portion of the gun is pulled back in order to eject an empty or jammed cartridge case.

BLM Chicago does not mention justice for the off-duty fireman who was beaten by the mob.

DISCUSSION.

There was no evidence to suggest that Joshua Beal's death was racially motivated. All evidence shows that he was killed while attempting to fire a gun at police officers.

LAMAR HARRIS. (4)

On March 14, 2016, Chicago Police Officers fatally shot Lamar Harris after Harris fired a weapon at the officers.

Harris was a known gang member who had been convicted seven times, including five felonies and two misdemeanors, according to Chicago Police. He has been arrested a total of 43 times, police said. His latest felony conviction came in 2012, when he was charged with aggravated, unlawful use of a weapon and resisting an officer causing injury.

The officers were on a narcotics patrol when they chased Harris into a dark alley. Mr. Harris ignored an order to stop and, as officers continued towards him, Harris turned, pulled a weapon from his waistband and fired at the officers. The officers returned fire. Mr. Harris continued shooting as he advanced toward the officers but was shot numerous times and collapsed. Police recovered a semi-automatic handgun from the ground next to Harris.

One officer sustained a gunshot wound to his abdomen and back. Another officer sustained a gunshot wound to his right heel. A third officer sustained two bullet impacts to his ballistic vest at the upper right chest that did not penetrate his skin. Harris was pronounced dead at the scene.

BLM Chicago does not mention justice for the three officers who sustained gunshot wounds.

DISCUSSION.

There was no evidence to suggest that Lamar Harris's death was racially motivated. All evidence shows that he was killed by police while fleeing arrest and firing a **semi-automatic** handgun at them.

QUINTONIO LeGRIER. (5)

On December 26, 2015, Quintonio LeGrier was shot and killed by a Chicago Police Officer who responded with his partner to several 911 calls made from LeGrier's residence. An investigation into the death of LeGrier was conducted by the Independent Police Review Authority (IPRA) and the Federal Bureau of Investigation. Investigators interviewed approximately 85 witnesses, reviewed photographs of the scene, police reports, medical records, results of forensic examinations and recordings of all 911 calls and officer communications.

On the day of the shooting, Antonio LeGrier, Quintonio LeGrier's father, called 911 and told the dispatcher that his son was armed with a baseball bat and was trying to break down the door to get into Antonio's bedroom.

The officers entered the apartment building and went up the stairs onto the front landing. Quintonio LeGrier opened his apartment door on the floor above and ran down the stairs toward the landing where the officers were standing. LeGrier entered the landing wielding an aluminum baseball bat. As the officers backed up, LeGrier moved towards them with the aluminum baseball bat raised in both hands above his head.

The officers backed off the landing and began backing down the stairs they had just ascended. LeGrier continued to advance on the officers with the bat, now considered a deadly weapon, raised as if to strike. As the officers walked backward down the stairs, LeGrier suddenly closed the distance and one officer fired several times, fatally striking LeGrier.

LeGrier's family filed a wrongful death lawsuit seeking a $25 million-dollar settlement. In 2018, the judge involved in the case decided that, because the jury's ruling found that the officer had reacted out of a reasonable fear of harm or death, the man's family could not be awarded any money.

DISCUSSION.

There was no evidence to suggest that Quintonio LeGrier's death was racially motivated. All evidence shows that he was killed by police while steadily advancing upon them with a deadly weapon despite numerous commands to stop.

RICHARD GRIMES. (6)

On November 27, 2016 at approximately 11:27 p.m., several Chicago Police Officers responded to an attempted murder. Richard Grimes shot Ashley Williams, his 37-week pregnant girlfriend, in the stomach and neck. Grimes then fled the apartment with the gun while a neighbor called 911.

Two of the involved officers were seated in a marked squad car when Grimes walked toward them with a gun in his hand. As one of the officers exited the vehicle, Grimes fired his gun, grazing the left side of the officer's forehead. Grimes then fled through an alley. A squad car dash-camera captured this shooting.

Additional responding officers surrounded Grimes. Grimes pointed his handgun at the officers in front of him and then at officers closing in behind. Residents inside the building heard officers yelling at Grimes to put his gun down. Officers then fired, and Grimes was struck several times and fell to the ground. Grimes' Hi-Point 9mm semi-automatic was recovered next to his body.

Richard Grimes used deadly force against an officer to evade arrest after he committed the forcible felonies of attempt murder and intentional homicide of an unborn child.

BLM Chicago does not mention justice for the injured officer, the eight months pregnant woman or the murdered, unborn infant.

DISCUSSION.

There was no evidence to suggest that Richard Grime's death was racially motivated. All evidence shows that he was killed by police while fleeing arrest and firing a gun at police.

THURMAN REYNOLDS. (7)

On March 19, 2016, at approximately 5:00 a.m., a Chicago resident observed his vehicle being driven away from his residence at a high rate of speed by an unknown offender. He reported this car theft to the police.

At approximately 5:30 a.m., a separate resident observed an unfamiliar car parked at a neighboring residence. That resident called 911 and reported a possible break in. Multiple officers responded to investigate the burglary in progress. Officers saw that the vehicle parked at the residence was the one that had been stolen a half hour before. Officers also observed signs of forced entry to the residence.

Officers then observed the burglary suspect, Thurman Reynolds, inside the residence and armed with a firearm. Officers established a perimeter around the house and gave repeated verbal commands for Reynolds to exit and surrender.

As Reynolds exited through a window, officers told Reynolds to stop. When the officers attempted to subdue Reynolds, he resisted arrest. Reynolds produced his gun and fired multiple gunshots, striking Officer Tim Jones several times.

As Reynolds attempted to flee, he pointed the weapon and fired back in the direction of police officers. Multiple officers returned fire at Reynolds, striking him multiple times. He was pronounced dead on scene.

Officer Jones was rushed to the hospital in critical condition. He sustained gunshot wounds to his head, jaw and chest. His injuries caused permanent debility and required years of therapy. Officer Jones' badge was retired in 2020.

BLM Chicago does not mention justice for Officer Jones, who is Black.

DISCUSSION.

There was no evidence to suggest that Thurman Reynold's death was racially motivated. All evidence shows that he was killed by police while shooting at police.

DEREK LOVE. (8)

On July 21, 2016, three Chicago Police Officers were stopped by two women. The women told the officers that there was a man (later identified as Derek Love) who had been acting erratically in a nearby park.

The officers arrived at the park and observed Derek Love sitting on a bench. The officers asked Love to keep his hands visible. Love then stood up, reached into his rear waistband and pulled out a handgun. Love began waving the gun back and forth. The officers gave verbal commands for Love to drop the weapon. Instead, Love fired his weapon, striking one officer in the left leg.

All three officers returned fire, fatally striking Love. Officers recovered Love's weapon and found it had a live round in the chamber. The injured officer was transported to Northwestern Hospital and was treated for the gunshot wound to his left leg.

BLM Chicago does not mention justice for the officer who Jones shot.

DISCUSSION.

There was no evidence to suggest that Derek Love's death was racially motivated. All evidence shows that he was killed by police while firing a gun at them.

PIERRE LOURY. (9)

According to the Cook County, IL, State's Attorney official report, On April 11, 2016, Pierre Loury was shot and killed by Chicago Police Officer Sean Hitz after Loury pointed a firearm at the officer. The Independent Police Review Authority (IPRA) / Civilian Office of Police Accountability (COPA) Chicago Police Department (CPD) and the Federal Bureau of Investigation (FBI) conducted an investigation into Loury's death.

Police officers received radio dispatches indicating that there were shots fired from a black car. The officers then heard people yelling from two other vehicles. The officers then saw a third vehicle, a black Ford Taurus. The individuals in the first two vehicles indicated to the officers that the black Taurus was involved in the shooting.

The officers followed the Taurus with activated emergency lights. Before the Taurus came to a complete stop, Pierre Loury exited the passenger door ran from the vehicle. Officer Hitz pursued Loury on foot through a vacant lot. Loury then ran into an alley.

Officer Hitz drew his weapon, entered the alley and encountered Loury who was straddling a fence with his leg stuck on one side. Loury pulled out a gun but it dropped to the ground. When Officer Hitz gave verbal commands for Loury to show his hands, Loury did not comply. Loury then ripped his pants free of the fence, jumped down, grabbed the gun and pointed it at Officer Hitz. Officer Hitz fired two shots, one of which struck Loury in the chest causing a fatal wound.

Officers recovered a 9mm semi-automatic Glock handgun near Loury's body and a black magazine on the street where Loury exited the black Ford Taurus. A DNA profile on the magazine matched Pierre Loury's. Officers also recovered a 9mm cartridge case from the grocery store where the earlier shots had been reported. A ballistics evidence analyst concluded that this fired cartridge case matched the weapon recovered from Loury. Gunshot Residue (GSR) samples taken from both of Pierre Loury's hands were positive.

DISCUSSION.

There was no evidence to suggest that Pierre Loury's death was racially motivated. All evidence shows that he was killed by police while fleeing arrest and armed with a gun.

Critical Theory tells us that every interaction between individuals in society serves to either reinforce or damage that society's invisible system of oppression. BLM Chicago seems to have used Theory's either-or decision template as the sole criteria for justice versus injustice in each of the preceding cases. If an 'oppressed' person was killed by an agent of the 'system,' then obviously an injustice occurred.

In this way, Theory exonerates those who are clearly guilty – burglars, murderers and would be cop killers – and vilifies those who would serve the law and protect the innocent. Theory produces a twisted inversion of justice based solely on race, a cunning perversion of truth in favor of necessary lies.

Examining facts, even those facts as anguished as those above, helps us again see Critical Theory and its progeny, Systemic Racism and Identity Politics, as the destructive social ills that they are.

Question what you're told. Dig for facts. Decide for yourself.

Please note that this was random sample of the cases presented on BLM Chicago's 'Justice for Families' page. The only innocent persons killed included Bettie Jones, a bystander struck by police bullets as they fired upon Quintonio LeGrier, and the unborn infant shot by Richard Grimes. I did not review all of the many cases presented.

CHAPTER ELEVEN.
JACOB BLAKE.

The following details were drawn from the *Report on the Officer Involved Shooting of Jacob Blake.* (1)

According to a report from the Cook County Sheriff's Department, on August 5, 2010 at 12:40 am in Des Plaines, IL, Jacob Blake was in a vehicle that had been stopped by a sheriff's deputy. During the traffic stop, Jacob Blake and another passenger exited the vehicle and approached the deputy. The deputy ordered Jacob Blake and the other passenger to get back inside the vehicle, but they refused. The deputy drew his weapon and Jacob Blake and the passenger retreated back inside the vehicle as backup arrived.

After the backup officer arrived, Jacob Blake again exited the vehicle. Both deputies attempted to secure Jacob Blake and a struggle ensued. Jacob Blake became combative and attempted to resist. As one of the deputies struggled to maintain control of Mr. Blake, Blake reached near his waistline with his left hand and produced a buck knife with a three-inch blade. Jacob Blake slashed at one deputy with the knife as the other deputy jumped back shouting, "knife, knife, knife." Both deputies unholstered their firearms. Jacob Blake then waved the knife around and advanced towards the officers while shouting, "Come on and shoot me then."

More law officers arrived and commanded Jacob Blake to drop the knife. Mr. Blake refused and was subsequently tased. Even after being tased, Mr. Blake actively resisted as officers attempted to take him into custody. Mr. Blake was tased again and the officers were able to subdue him.

A few years later, on May 3, 2020, the Kenosha Police Department took a report from Laquisha

Booker. Ms. Booker stated that Jacob Blake had broken into her residence, sexually assaulted her and then stolen her car keys, her vehicle and her debit card. Jacob Blake was charged with Criminal Trespass, Domestic Abuse, Third Degree Sexual Assault and Disorderly Conduct. The charges were filed on July 6, 2020 and a warrant was issued for Jacob Blake's arrest.

Laquisha Booker had called the police regarding domestic disputes with Jacob Blake numerous times over the prior eight years. Ms. Booker had reported that Jacob Blake hit her, choked her, and, on May 3, 2020, that he sexually assaulted her. Four of Ms. Booker's calls to the police involved disputes over vehicles. According to one police report in 2012, Ms. Booker reported that Jacob Blake had domestically assaulted her and then, as the police responded, he wrestled her keys away and sped off in her car, fleeing from police, and then crashed her car.

On July 14, 2020, Jacob Blake sent Laquisha Booker a text that read, "Just tell him you don't remember what you said and you would like to drop the charges." Several hours later, Mr. Blake sent another text stating, "[I]f I'm willing to take them to the park and I got a whole arrest warrant you can't tell me that you can't get up and take them to a park....I rather take the chance."

Jacob Blake's cell phone history showed internet searches on August 7, 2020 and again on August 9, 2020, when he looked up his pending warrant case in online court records.

In spite of this history, Laquisha Booker said she had allowed Jacob Blake to be at her residence on

August 23, 2020, so they could celebrate their son's birthday.

On August 23, 2020, Kenosha, WI, police officers responded to a 'family trouble' call which they knew was between Laquisha Booker and the father of her children, Jacob Blake. It was unclear if Laquisha Booker was in a relationship with Jacob Blake at the time of this incident, but they had three children together. According to Mr. Blake's subsequent statement, Laquisha Booker was angry with him because he did not seem more upset when he found out that she had been sleeping with the neighbor's husband.

Ms. Booker stated that Jacob Blake had taken the keys to her rental vehicle which he would not return to her. Ms. Booker added that she was afraid that Jacob Blake was going to take her vehicle and crash it as, she stated, he had done before. In her 911 called, Ms. Booker stated, "He's crashed numerous of my vehicles in the past and I literally just bought one like yesterday. And so, just because he heard some false information, he's not willing to give me the keys to this car that doesn't even belong to me."

Dispatch informed the responding officers that Jacob Blake had "a 99," meaning a warrant (in this case a felony warrant for his arrest from a prior incident where he was charged with domestic violence offenses and a sexual assault). Therefore, responding officers knew that they would have to arrest Jacob Blake if they encountered him, regardless of whatever else might happen.

When officers arrived, Laquisha Booker flagged them down, identified Jacob Blake as the other person involved in the dispute and indicated that he was

149

trying to take her car. She stated, "My kids are in the car."

As outlined above, Jacob Blake clearly knew there was an active warrant out for his arrest.

When the officers approached Mr. Blake, he refused to comply with their verbal commands as they attempted to arrest him. When the officers attempted to physically restrain Jacob Blake, he resisted, struggling with officers. The officers brought Mr. Blake to the ground, but he was able to get back up. Both officers deployed their tasers during this struggle, and both times he was hit Mr. Blake ripped out the taser prongs.

As he walked away from the officers, Mr. Blake was armed with a knife. By the time he was walking in front of the SUV, the knife was open, and the blade was exposed. The officers shouted for Mr. Blake to drop the knife but he refused.

As Mr. Blake tried to enter the driver's door of the Ms. Booker's SUV, he was pulled backward by one officer who had grabbed Mr. Blake's shirt. Mr. Blake had the opened knife in his right hand while attempting to escape from the officer's grasp. A civilian cellphone video captured a male voice saying 'Drop the knife' at least twice.

At this point the responding officers knew that Jacob Blake was armed, resisting arrest, unaffected by escalating non-lethal methods (verbal commands, physical restraint and the tazer blasts), had an active felony warrant and appeared to be about to flee in a stolen vehicle which contained at least one child.

Both of the officers and two civilian witnesses saw Mr. Blake twist his body and move his right hand with the knife towards the closest officer. At that point, the officer released Mr. Blake's shirt and triggered his firearm. The officer fired until Mr. Blake dropped the knife. This required seven shots in rapid succession.

After the shooting, investigators recovered a knife from the driver's side floorboard of the SUV. When the knife was recovered the blade was out (the knife was open). When later shown a photo of this knife, Jacob Blake verified it was his knife.

Jacob Blake specifically told investigators in his September 21 interview that he did not know there was an arrest warrant for him in the system.

Again, these are the facts outlined in Kenosha County District Attorney Michael Graveley's *Report on the Officer Involved Shooting of Jacob Blake Synopsis*.

What happened before these facts were understood?

The shooting was captured by a neighbor in a video that quickly went viral on social media.

Almost immediately after this shooting, Democratic Wisconsin Governor Tony Evers Tweeted, "Tonight, Jacob Blake was shot in the back multiple times, in broad daylight, in Kenosha."

The Governor added, "While we do not have all of the details yet, what we know for certain is that he is not the first Black man or person to have been shot or injured or mercilessly killed at the hands of individuals in law enforcement in our state or our country."

Evers added that he stood "with all those who have and continue to demand justice, equity, and accountability for Black lives in our country" and "against excessive use of force and immediate escalation when engaging with Black Wisconsinites."

Governor Evers admitted that he lacked the details of this case but proceeded to inaccurately portray the officers' actions merciless, unjust and excessive.

In a Tweet on August 24, 2020, Democratic Massachusetts Rep. Joe Kennedy III tweeted that Blake's shooting was typical of the "police brutality and white supremacy" in the country.

An August 24, 2020 *Washington Post* article written by Eugene Robinson (2) stated Jacob Blake "is not seen [in the video] to brandish or even possess any kind of weapon. Yet the officers already have their guns drawn and aimed at his back. The only threat we see being presented, the only crime we see being committed, is Blake's brown skin."

Mr. Robinson finishes with, "This is why the Black Lives Matter movement exists — and why it must persist. As long as there are police forces that act like armies of occupation rather than guardians of public safety, as long as there are officers who see the people who live in the communities they patrol as criminals rather than citizens, protesters will have to take to the streets."

People did take to the streets just as the hasty and ignorant but passionate Eugene Robinson had encouraged. That night, rioters set fires that destroyed the Kenosha Probation and Parole Building and a business called B & L Furniture. Those arsons were among several buildings, and dozens of vehicles, set ablaze during riots August 23 through 25.

Misinformed, purposefully manipulated and misdirected outrage spread quickly. In the nights that followed, demonstrators burned buildings and cars and threw fireworks, water bottles and bricks at police officers in riot gear. Protests spread across the country, to cities including Madison, Portland, Minneapolis and New York.

Too impatient for actual facts, players from the National Basketball Association, the WNBA, the National Football League, Major League Baseball, Major League Soccer and other pro sports settled for obtuse opinions and staged hasty boycotts. On August 26, 2020, a statement from Milwaukee Bucks players showed their faith in false narratives by "calling for justice for Jacob Blake and demand the officers be held accountable." An ESPN2 broadcast showed WNBA players locked arm in arm while kneeling and wearing shirts spelling out Jacob Blake's name.

The Baltimore Ravens added to this swirling torrent of ignorant misinformation on August 27 when their website stated, "With yet another example of racial discrimination with the shooting of Jacob Blake, and the unlawful abuse of peaceful protesters, we MUST unify as a society." Perhaps the Ravens had discovered some peaceful rioters that were peacefully burning building and cars and while peacefully assaulting in Kenosha.

The Ravens also called for the officers involved in both the Jacob Blake and the Breonna Taylor incidents be arrested and charged. Unsurprisingly, they did not make clear any compelling legal case for doing so. To this writer's knowledge, they also never offered retractions or apologies to those officers once the truth was made public.

An August 27 Twitter statement including the BLM hashtag and those of the NFL and the NFL players' association stated, "We share anger and frustration, most recently as a result of the shooting of Jacob Blake." The statement added that they "are proud that our players and clubs, League and Union, are taking time to have the difficult conversations about these issues." These conversations were no doubt made less difficult by the absence of any messy and confusing facts.

A September 4, 2020, CNN article (4) quoted Alexis Hoag, lecturer and associate research scholar at Columbia Law School. "What's so striking about Kenosha is that it put this racial inequality in sharp relief." Hoag added, "What is left unaddressed is this presumption of dangerousness and criminality that society -- it's bigger than law enforcement -- assigns to Black people" and "That is a direct descendant of the racial hierarchy that formed during slavery."

Of course, the officers in Blake's case had no reason to presume dangerousness or criminality, as Ms. Hoag claims. These officers knew Mr. Blake had an active arrest warrant for his criminal behavior and responded to Blake's dangerous actions.

This was, of course, just two weeks after the shooting and Ms. Hoag was nearly as ignorant of the details as Mr. Eugene Robinson. Both Ms. Hoag and Mr. Robinson, presumably educated and articulate people, assumed some racial motivation. Then they spewed forth their pseudo-intellectual assumptions.

This arrogant drivel likely fueled the ongoing racially charged unrest.

I suspect Ms. Hoag, an academic, is a Critical Theory cultist as evidenced by her focus the flaws in America's past and the mention of 'racial hierarchy.' Neither Hoag nor Robinson offered any supporting evidence of their claims and, to my knowledge, never offered any retraction when their words were proven wrong.

In fact, none of the individuals or organizations who jumped to ignorant conclusions ever apologized to the police officers who were vilified in the media for months. There is no consequence for having done so. These brave officers responded to the call of a woman in distress, attempted to arrest a known offender on a felony warrant for sexual assault and resorted to lethal force only as the very last of an escalating series of attempts that the armed suspect forcefully resisted. These officers were cast as 'racist' agents of 'white supremacy.'

That is the disgusting but true narrative that sociologists and activists and the media collectively ignore as they perpetuate false narratives in the name of Theory.

On January 5, 2021, the BLM Global Network released their response to the Wisconsin District Attorney's decision not to charge the officer who shot Jacob Blake Shooting. (5) It stated, "It comes as no surprise that Kenosha police officer Rusten Sheskey was not charged for his attempted murder of Jacob Blake, because there is no criminal justice system that works for Black people, and there is no safety or justice in America for Black people." Sadly, this once again demonstrates BLM Global Network's dismissal of facts in favor of their preferred narrative.

The response continued, "District Attorney Graveley had the opportunity to provide justice for Jacob and his family but has instead chosen to fuel the racially charged agenda to overpolice and criminalize Black people in America." As always, 'justice' goes undefined in BLM's racially charged agenda to the villainize police who, fully in line with their dangerous duty, reacted to Mr. Blake's criminal behavior. BLM certainly must have a very low opinion of their followers to keep shoveling this falsified rubbish into their faces.

In March 2021, Jacob Blake filed a civil suit against the officer who shot him.

12. DISCUSSION.

The primary differences between Critical Theory and classic liberal thought include:

CRITIAL THEORY:	LIBERAL THOUGHT:
Focused on past wrongs.	Focused on future opportunity.
Focused on finding problems.	Focused on finding solutions.
Seeks to divide.	Seeks to unify.
Stifles opposing views.	Encourages new ideas.
Restricts 'acceptable' language.	Promotes free expression.
Confined to rigid assumptions.	Expands boundaries of thought.

Promotes false narratives.	Promotes factual reason.
Leads to inflexible demands.	Supports creative negotiation.
Inherently pessimistic.	Cautiously optimistic.

Critical Theory is not truth. Critical Theory is one way we can chose to look at the world around us. It is by no means the best way.

Critical Theory and its diseased children (Systemic Racism, the intersecting traumas of Identity Politics, White Supremacy, etc.) promote false narratives and outright lies. They have no firm foundation of reproducible evidence or sustainable reason. Like cognitive vampires, they feed on and are sustained by our hate, fear, division and suspicion.

Why do smart people believe in and perpetuate social corruptions like eugenics and Critical Theory?

Critical Theory is deceptively simple. It is easy to imagine an oppressive hierarchy. It is easier and more comfortable to adopt a belief in Systemic Racism than it is to parse through the many possible (and often uncomfortable) reasons for disparities between various groups.

We look for things that easily reinforce what we already believe. This is 'confirmation bias.' When the media tells us that Jacob Blake is the next example of White violence against Blacks, it seems to confirm what we believe about racism. We like things that make us feel right, things that confirm we are smart and insightful.

Social Media impedes insightful conversation. Twitter limits you to 280 characters. Longer Facebook posts get less attention than memes. People state their opinions as facts and rarely ask questions or for clarification. Posting popular opinions for 'Likes' feels good. Even feuds, trollings and rants make us feel alive (angry, but alive).

The corporate media reinforces the narrative. Think back on the media coverage in Ferguson in 2014. Review the news surrounding Breonna Taylor's tragedy. We live in an age where we anticipate that journalists are biased (at least the ones on the 'other' side). We don't hold news reporters or news makers to any standard of accountability. We're ceaselessly bombarded with fictions that look indistinguishable from truth. These fictions usually are distinguishable, though this takes significant personal effort.

There is no competing narrative that is as compelling. Maybe you reject Postmodern Critical Theory. But what do you take up in its place? Some hazy status quo seems inadequate. Alt-Right narratives are equally vile. This leaves many well-intentioned people without an ideologic home. Read on for suggestions to get past this.

There is a potential cost for voicing opposition. Questioning White Supremacy simply proves you're a White supremacist (or so the current thinking goes). JK Rowling supported a belief in the uniqueness of biological females and was instantly crucified in the media for her 'trans phobia.' No one wants to be the next one shamed, cancelled and potentially fired.

Stories affect us more than facts. The story of Breonna Taylor as a simple, sweet, model citizen who was gunned down by racist cops triggers strong emotions. People tend to like strong emotions. They make us feel alive. Better still are strong emotions shared in like-minded groups (in things like street protests or online forums). Emotions are sexy. Facts are boring.

We have an innate need for control. The media would have us believe that our world is in chaos. Racism is rampant and innocent People of Color are being intentionally gunned down. We regain a sense of control in this 'chaos' by adopting a plausible explanation. Systemic Racism offers that structure (even as it reinforces the very same chaos).

We have an innate need to belong. From knitting circles to street gangs, all of us want the positive reinforcement that comes with group affiliation. Our current Social Justice warriors offer the chance to be involved in an exciting group. Wrongheaded and toxic, but exciting.

It's hard to admit that you're wrong. The Cult of Critical Theory is seductively easy to join. Once in that toxic quagmire of blame and trauma, it's hard to escape. Our powerful American egos make it difficult to admit to ourselves when we've joined the wrong team.

Systemic Racism and Critical Theory are so vague they're hard to argue against. In the absence of a valid counter-argument (hopefully this book serves the purpose), many might simply go along.

Critical Theory is just an idea. It is one way to view society. Since it is not 'true' it cannot be proven 'false.' When many seemingly credible people state that its true, it becomes easy to accept as such.

There is peer pressure. Critical Theory is currently a fashionable narrative. Many people passionately believe in it (or at least enjoy riding its wave of popularity). These people can exert social pressure to join the movement.

The authority of so-called experts is compelling. If a published PhD or the President says something is true, we're likely to believe it.

Many people don't immediately look for underlying agendas. I believe most people are optimists. Many assume others are acting on benevolent intentions. Many believe they are truthful until proven otherwise. Critical Theory was intended to be political. Its agenda has become toxic.

We are cognitive misers. We like mental shortcuts and predictable patterns and things that allow us to focus on what we enjoy. Whatever spares us precious mental energy is good. Once we've adopted a social concept, we no longer need to invest further thought into it.

There is no lie so powerful as the lie we tell our self. Many people simply chose to keep believing in Critical Theory (and Systemic Racism, White Supremacy, Identity Politics, etc.) *despite* overt evidence that counters the false narratives that support it. Keen introspection is a very rare skill. The ugly stains on our souls are easier to paint over than to clean. It seems better to maintain a comforting fiction than to confront a terrible truth.

These are all possibilities. My theory? I believe that we are too comfortable near the top of Maslow's Hierarchy of needs. Too complacent. Too bored. Too purposeless.

Abraham Maslow argued that humans act upon several basic motivations. At the bottom of his pyramid was basic survival. Sating hunger. Quenching thirst. Escaping extremes of heat and cold.

My very dear friend's father was a child in Nazi Germany. This man, Julius, once relayed the story of a Nazi transport moving through his town. The transport stopped and a prisoner, an emaciated figure in rags, broke free of the convoy and sprinted toward a woman holding a basket of vegetables. Reaching her, he grabbed an onion and began devouring it in manic haste. This person suffered such extreme starvation that he risked Nazi clubs and bullets for food. That is the bottom of Maslow's hierarchy. There we sacrifice physical safety for our body's immediate physiologic demands.

Maslow's mid-level motivations include basic physical safety and socio-economic security. These include such things as housing, a reliable income and the means to maintain health. Things that maintain our basic existence. Just above this are close relationships that meet our needs for interpersonal connection.

Near the top of this pyramid are existential motivations. The need to feel respected, admired and accomplished. The desire to fulfill personal ambitions that give our unique being a sense of completion. We reach the apex of 'self-actualization' when feel we have attained these topmost desires.

And there's the rub. We are victims of our own success. Too many of us exist in comfortable, complacent convenience.

A fellow physician from India once told me what it was like to come as an adult to the United States. He and his wife had practiced medicine in India before starting over in America. They lived in a home that only sporadically had hot water. They often conducted their medical clinics by candlelight due to random power outages. And they were the fortunate people.

He had always heard about a place called Starbucks. When he arrived in the US this was one of his first stops. He recalled waiting to order. Finally, when it was his turn, he requested one of their famous coffees. The staggering number of options made this very educated and successful Indian man literally "want to cry." He had to excuse himself from the front of the line.

Those of us who take our Starbucks and cellphones for granted, or even feel outraged when service is even briefly interrupted, are living unaware at the top of Maslow's hierarchy. But where do we go from there? So many battles have already been fought and our personal comfort and convenience have been secured.

The French call it ennui. A state of empty, tedious intellectual doldrums. A painful existential crisis of conscious. The uncomfortable awareness of a lack definite purpose.

This existential void is too painful to continue, so we fill it with something. Anything. And what is both widely available and fashionable? Critical Theory. Critical Theory, as exampled throughout this book, requires no uncomfortable critical thinking to employ. It is a vapid ideology for lazy minds. It is a convenient idea for people deeply embedded in their own comfortable convenience.

I believe Critical Theory, Systemic Racism, White Privilege, Identity Politics and all the divisive harm they inflict are fueled by this gnawing collective cognitive angst. There are very real problems with inter-group disparities, to be sure. But there are very real problems in every area of human existence – racial, philosophical, governmental, theological, ecological, etc., etc., etc. With no obvious and convenient outlet for our existential angst, we turn to Critical Theory and begin to destroy each other and thus ourselves.

As an optimist tackling an inherently pessimistic subject, I believe we can do better.

13. HOW TO FIX THINGS.

GOALS AND SOLUTIONS.

The solutions that follow are my own daydreams about what our country could do. I admittedly have no background in drafting public policy. They are ideas that might help decrease the racial disparities that exist in the United States.

After such a lengthy examination of Critical Theory's hateful pessimism, I feel that offering solutions, any solutions, even if they are deemed bad or hopelessly naïve solutions, was better than offering no solutions.

Any possible solution should be judged by certain criteria. What is the specific underlying goal? What definable problem are you trying to solve? If you can't answer that, pause.

Next, ask if your goal is based on a practical ideology. Let's say that your goal is to correct the disparity of under-represented Amish people in CEO positions. More specifically, you want to see ten percent of all CEO positions filled by Amish people.

This in an outcome goal as opposed to a process goal. A process goal might be to change the educational system in order to prepare Amish people better for CEO positions. It's important to know the difference.

This specific outcome goal, while perhaps well intentioned, is fatally flawed. Amish people do not want CEO positions. Their culture places no value on such things. They would be disinterested in your effort to help them achieve such a goal and your goal would fail. In this example, neither an outcome goal or a process goal would reach its desired end.

Definite outcome or process goals based on practical ideology should next be gauged for feasibility. Here we will use a modified 'SMART' goal technique. SMART is an acronym for specific, measurable, achievable, realistic and timely. We'll instead use 'STREAM" goals by adding an 'E' for economically feasible.

S: Is the goal Specific? Universal healthcare is not a specific goal. It is a broad ideology that can be broken down into many hundreds of specific goals. Improving cost-effective healthcare access and delivery to at-risk toddlers in rural New Mexico over the next 18 months is specific.

Similarly, ending Systemic Racism is not a specific goal. I will argue that activists do not want to make specific goals to end Systemic Racism. To do so, they would have to carefully and narrowly define it, which they cannot. They would then have to enter into conversations about cases like those we have covered. Cases where the false narrative of Systemic Racism can readily be dispelled.

T: Can the goal be accomplished in a Timely manner? Consider the War on Poverty, the War on Drugs and the War on Terrorism. These 'wars' can never be definitely concluded because poverty, drugs and terrorism will always exist. Reducing the rate of opiate abuse in Indianapolis by five percent over twelve months is a timely goal. It is also specific, relevant and perhaps achievable. Whether or not it is measurable and cost-effective depends on how the process is set up.

R: Is it Relevant? Any goal should address an actual, existing, definable problem. In the context of this book, ending Systemic Racism is not a relevant goal because Systemic Racism does not exist. Now, some might try to twist this paragraph by claiming, 'the author says racism is irrelevant!' That is not true. Racism and its effects are extremely relevant. Achieving specific goals that reduce disparities will decrease racist beliefs and actions.

E: Is it Economically feasible? The goal should be realistically accomplished with the finite resources available. The cost of the goal should also be measured against the opportunity cost of abandoning other goals. Creative problems solvers can often increase a pie before it is sliced, but there is no infinite pie.

A: Is it Achievable? Return to our dear Amish friends. My father was Amish until he was in third grade, by the way. Getting ten percent of CEO positions filled by Amish people is not achievable because these people don't want or value the outcome.

M: Is it Measurable? Much of Big Government's legislation consists of grandiose ideas that win hearts but lacks minds. These are huge policy initiatives whose real effects cannot be properly measured. This might be because such measurable effects were not built in, the government lacks the ability to measure or because policy makers do not want the outcomes true revealed. A good goal is a measurable goal.

Returning to the theme of this book, Systemic Racism cannot be measured. Many will point to specific data regarding educational, professional and health outcomes as true measurements of Systemic Racism. But again, any possible correlation does not equal causation. Disparities in health outcomes can be due in part to regional dietary preferences, for example. Many, many variables play into such disparities. Ignoring these real variables in favor of attribution to an elusive boogeyman is, quite bluntly, a stupid approach to complex problems.

Note that the following solutions are very broad and can be broken down into several 'STREAM' goals. These broad solutions are simply more readable and wile any specific goals are beyond the reach of this book. These are only a few of the solutions that occurred to me while writing this book. Some are not new ideas, but simply old ideas that can be aptly applied.

VOTE WITH YOUR DOLLARS.

Direct your spending toward products and companies that promote universal humanity (or at least don't bow down at the unholy alter of Critical Theory). Unsubscribe to newspapers, magazines and websites spew Theory-minded nonsense. Contribute to the campaigns of sensible, fact-minded candidates who reject Theory's devilish progeny (Systemic Racism, Identity Politics, etc.).

REFORM PUBLIC SCHOOL TEACHER DISMISSAL.

Private sector unions negotiate for shares of earned profits. Public sector teachers' unions negotiate for percentages of tax revenue. This means there are no competitive pressures limiting how much they can demand. Teachers' unions negotiate directly with elected officials who they often help elect. This puts the interests of public sector unions in direct conflict with taxpayer interests. Elected officials, wary of these unions' massive media and campaign budgets, are under tremendous pressure to meet these demands.

The two largest teacher's unions in the US are The American Federation of Teachers (AFT) and the National Education Association (NEA). Both span the US and have enormous lobbying footprints in Washington DC. With their vast financial reserves, both are also deeply entangled with state and local level elections. If you have free time, log on to the website of Influence Watch and do some investigating.

These unions help preserve teacher "tenure" policies that make it exceptionally inefficient and prohibitively costly to remove ineffective teachers from the classroom. What is the alternative?

Consider the way that medical malpractice claims are handled in Indiana. Once a malpractice suit is filed, either side of the dispute can ask to have a medical review panel formed to investigate the merits of the case (if neither side asks, no panel is formed). Note that the side that 'wins' the dispute must pay the panel's fee, which in 2020 averaged about $3,000.

The panel consists of one attorney (representing neither side) and three impartial health care providers. The Indiana Department of Insurance, which might have a conflict of interest in any given case, has no role in the panel's selection process. The attorney acts as chair of the panel and in an advisory capacity but has no vote. The panel then reviews all evidence provided and renders an opinion within a specified time frame. Compensation for the panel members is set within a maximum limit.

The panel's decision essentially serves as an 'expert opinion' about how the case would likely be decided if it proceeded to court. If the physician's care was deemed within the standard of care, the claimant is very unlikely to press ahead with the case, given the cost of doing so and the low chance of success. Conversely, if the physician was found in error, they are much more likely to settle out of court. Either way, both sides save the enormous amount of time and money involved in a full court hearing.

Similarly, an educational review panel could be formed for teachers accused of incompetence or misconduct. Either the school (or school board) or the teacher could ask for a panel to be formed. The panel could be composed of an attorney or licensed

169

mediator and impartial three teachers. Teachers' unions, with potential conflicts of interest, would be excluded from the panel's selection process.

Of course, teaching and medicine are two very different beasts. The panel process for teachers and schools would have to be tailored for the realities of teacher and student safety and the peculiarities of teachers' contracts and school administration policies. But, as with any issue, creative and mutually beneficial solutions could abound. Maybe the panel has five members. Maybe the panel includes a PTA member. Maybe two panels convene in tandem to see if they reach the same conclusion.

As with medicine, both time and money could be saved (time and money that could be better used in the classroom). In this way, all school would have more resources.

SUPPORT CREATIVE (AND DATA DRIVEN) TEACHING MODELS.

Even a casual stroll through the vast forest of research on education suggest several ways to improve school performance for minority students. The following suggestions are based on that evidence. Consider that, by some estimates, every potential high school drop out that gets a high school diploma saves taxpayers $100,000. Everyone wins when Black and Latino students excel.

First, create financial incentives for longitudinal teaching for at-risk minority students. Some evidence indicates that a high performing teacher involved with at-risk students at the earliest ages can have significant, long term positive effects. This teacher would engage children in kindergarten or first grade and remain as their teacher each year for four years as they progress to third or fourth grade.

Create financial incentives to promote demographically paired teaching. Evidence suggests that young Black learners paired with Black teachers do better in both the short and long term. Getting more Black teachers into predominantly Black elementary school classrooms could improve outcomes.

INSIST ON INCLUSIVE SCHOOLS, NOT ACTIVIST SCHOOLS.

Critical Theory is increasingly poisoning our children's minds. The NEA wants Critical Race Theory and Critical Gender Theory in classrooms. Tell them no. If a classroom topic is not pure education, it is likely indoctrination.

Meet with your school's diversity officer (if they exist) and discover their views on Critical Theory. Attend School Board meetings and push back against Theory-based proposals. Cite this book if it helps.

WEEKEND MEALS FOR HUNGRY KIDS.

Promote weekend meals for at risk students. Many children face 'food insecurity,' or inadequate and unpredictable access to nutrition. Some enjoy subsidized breakfast and lunch at school but arrive unready to learn on Monday mornings due to hunger. At the same time, many schools have excess unused food on Friday afternoons that cannot be used the following week. Make this food available for parents to pick up or arrange to have it sent home with children.

GET PHYSICIANS INVOLVED.

Many physicians have opportunities to get books into the hands of at-risk minority parents and children. Offer no-cost books to new parents before they take their newborn home. Offer more age appropriate books at each well child check while stressing the importance of reading to children at home. While I'd love to see some Play-Doh thrown in as well, there's probably no data to support it.

UNIVERSAL POLICE BODY CAMERAS.

Imagine how differently events in Ferguson would have unfolded had Officer Wilson had body camera video when he encountered Michael Brown. If the public could have seen the interaction as it actually occurred, much misery could have been avoided.

While the physical and financial resources in such a case are secondary considerations, they remain consequential. Body camera video could have quickly negated the need for long and costly investigations by

the Ferguson police department and the federal
Justice Department.

FUNDING METHOD 1. TAX CIGARETTES OUT OF EXISTNCE.

Tobacco is an addictive, carcinogenic weed. If anyone tried to introduce it as a viable product today, they'd be rejected for a thousand reasons.

Every day I step into the hospital, I see tobacco related illness. It is the great scourge on American health. COPD. Cancer. Heart disease. Peripheral vascular disease. In my experience, nothing else comes close to the damage caused by cigarettes to an individual's wellness.

The cost to society is beyond enormous. According to drugabuse.gov, between 2009 and 2012, the annual costs to US taxpayers were between $289 and $332.5 billion. This includes $132.5 to $175.9 billion for direct medical care of adults and $151 billion for lost productivity due to premature deaths. These costs far exceed any tax revenue generated by tobacco sales.

Blacks smoke cigarettes at slightly higher rates than Whites, and southerners smoke more than northerners. Menthol cigarettes have typically been marketed to urban Blacks. About three in four Black smokers use menthol cigarettes (more than three times the rate of Whites menthol smokers). The menthol in these cigarettes makes it harder to quit smoking.

An average pack of cigarettes in the US is six dollars (a low estimate). The current federal tax is a dollar. State taxes vary widely, but the actual pre-tax cost of a pack of cigarettes is about four dollars. I propose making the federal tax rate twice the average actual cost of a pack of cigarettes. If pre-tax cigarettes cost $4, the federal tax would be $8, making the pack cost $12 (before the states added their taxes).

A prohibitively high federal tax rate would discourage illegal inter-state sales and smuggling, because no state would have affordable cigarettes.

At the same time, we can protect those who can least afford their addiction to tobacco. While tobacco would be legal to buy, we can make it illegal for retailers to sell tobacco products to anyone receiving any form of state welfare assistance (such information would be embedded on the potential buyer's driver's license).

Such measures would:

Decrease cigarette consumption. Public tax revenue would decrease but public taxpayer expenditures on smoking related health problems would also decrease. The health benefits from decreased smoking would negate much of the lost productivity and premature death.

Decreased cigarette consumption would also put about $180 dollars a month back into any former one-pack-per-day smoker's budget. These same ex-smokers would also have fewer (or perhaps never incur the inevitable) smoking-related healthcare expenses (medications, clinic visits, emergency department visits, hospital stays, etc.)

FUNDING METHOD 2. LEGALIZE IT.

I'm not a marijuana user. That stated, I've never seen a single marijuana-related health crisis in my decade as a hospitalist. I've never admitted a frequent or even chronic marijuana user with problems directly attributable from this drug. I was fortunate enough to have a conversation with a former US Surgeon General about marijuana. Their only argument against legalization was the potential difficulty in quantifying each strain's potency.

Some estimate that policing marijuana possession costs US taxpayers over $3 billion dollars every year and leads to hundreds of thousands of annual arrests. All of these individuals incur both court costs and lost revenue while processing their case and any jail time incurred.

If these people are convicted of marijuana related offenses, some estimates say their lifetime wage potential is cut down more than 25%.

Legalize marijuana at the federal level.

Legal marijuana would:

One: Save the vast amount of money spent nationally on policing, prosecuting and jailing people for marijuana related offenses. Public costs go down.

Two: Allow us to tax marijuana sales. Public funds go up.

Three: Allow us to release those in jail simply for marijuana related offenses. Public costs (of ongoing incarceration) go down.

For those released from prison for simple marijuana offenses, clear these offenses from their records. These people return to the work force. Public productivity goes up. The damaging effect of a criminal record goes down.

Four: Potentially have an immediate and significant impact on the 'opiate crisis.'

Legal marijuana use would likely lead to less opiate abuse. The cost of policing, prosecuting and jailing people for opiate related offenses. Public costs go down.

With less opiate abuse, the public cost of medically treating the consequences of opiate abuse (such as unintentional overdoses) becomes less. Public cost goes down.

Five: Allow us to dedicate 50% of this new federal marijuana tax revenue to under-funded, predominantly Black and Latino schools for a period of thirty years. Dedicate another 25% to rehabilitation programs for People of Color affected by drugs, alcohol or prior incarceration for the same period.

Six: Allow us to align federal resources with the poor tobacco farmers we've just put out of business. Marijuana can be their new cash crop (under federal surveillance).

But isn't marijuana a 'gateway drug?' Only because users need drug dealers to get marijuana. Legal marijuana retail shops would be as drug-dealer free as any tobacco shop.

But won't Big Pharma and Big Tobacco push back with their billion-dollar lobbying war chest? Probably. That's where the integrity of our policy makers comes in. These people answer to you. That's why your vote still matters.

SOLUTIONS COMPARED TO DEMANDS.

Too many of the so-called leaders in today's activist community simply shout out lists of demands. We've seen several examples already.

BLM Global Network South Bend demanded the officer who fatally shot Eric Logan be fired and charged with murder. This goal was specific, timely, economically possible, achievable and measurable. But it was not 'relevant' in the sense that no murder was committed.

The Milwaukee Bucks called for justice for Jacob Blake and demanded the officers be held accountable. They defined neither justice nor accountability, so this was not specific. Being unspecific, it could neither be measured nor realistically achieved in any timely manner. And, like the tragedy of Eric Logan, it lacked true criminal relevance.

The main BLM Global Network website posted "BLM's 7 Demands." They demanded an investigation into the White Supremacy in law enforcement and the military because "police departments have been a safe haven for white supremacists to hide malintent behind a badge, because the badge was created for that purpose."

Consider BLM Chicago's "10 Demands of BLMCHI." These included literally defunding of the entire Chicago police Department and the immediate closure of Cook County's juvenile detention center.

BLM Houston called for immediately freeing all people from 'involuntary confinement,' including jails, prisons, immigrant detention centers and psychiatric facilities. They also demanded permanently closure local jails.

BLM Los Angeles created a list of "Black Los Angeles Demands in Light of COVID-19 and Rates of Black Death" dated April 16, 2020. These included fifty-one separate demands including:

Income supplement of $2000 per month per adult and $1000 per month per child for all Black residents.

A complete moratorium on all non-violent arrests and immediate dismissal of all non-violent criminal warrants and citations.

Cancellation of rents and mortgages.

Reparations for all Black victims of COVID-19 or their families in cases of death due to "overall medical racism."

Guaranteed admission to and scholarships for Black students to all public colleges and universities.

"On-demand," free housing for homeless people.

"On-demand," free medical care.

Free food.

Free public transportation.

Free housing.

Free public transportation.

Free childcare.

Free burial/cremation services for COVID-19 deaths.

Again, think of goals that are specific, timely, relevant, economically feasible, achievable and measurable. Toddlers and bank robbers can make demands. Adults who want to achieve real progress first create clear goals and then propose specific solutions. If someone approaches you with demands (recall the 24 Hour Fitness scenario), tell them that if they want to talk with the grownups, they need to talk like a grownup.

14. FINALLY (ALMOST).

Critical Theory is a theory. It is not fact. It is one way to philosophically examine the world. There are other ways to do so. Identity Politics, Systemic Racism and White Supremacy are byproducts of Critical Theory. These too are not facts. They are the constructs of sociologists.

Everyone is well within their rights to deny that Critical Theory is the necessary lens to view the world through. Anyone can instead employ classic, reason-based liberal thought and a world view that underscores the universal worth and humanity of everyone.

Continue to look for the truth behind the fictions and facades. While you do so, continue asking these questions.

Is this true?

Is this Constitutional?

Is this Biblical? Or, if you're not of the Christian faith, ask whether it insults your soul's fixed moral code. If you lack a fixed moral code, get to Church.

Does this reinforce everyone's shared humanity?

Does this eagerly invite probing questions and doubts?

Does this stand up to close factual investigation?

What is the agenda behind this?

What are the short-term consequences of this? The long-term consequences? The unintended consequences?

Do I want my children to believe this?

Does this have a definite goal that supports realistic solutions?

THANK YOU!

If you've read this far, you have my appreciation. I sincerely hope that you, dear Reader, feel more informed and more able to engage in civil, civic discussions.

We live in a fascinating age where ideas can spread instantaneously via social media. If you found this book valuable, please share it with others who might benefit from a unique perspective.

If you have feedback (let's keep it classy) or questions, send me an email:

cult.of.critical.theory@gmail.com

Sincerely,

DR. DM SCHWARTZ, MD, MBA

NOTES.

CHAPTER 1. WHAT CRITICAL RACE THEORY IS AND ISN'T.

1 The Causes of Race Superiority. Edward A. Ross. The Annals of the American Academy of Social Science. Volume 18. July, 1901. Pages 67-89.

https://www.jstor.org/stable/1009883?seq=1#metadata_info_t ab_contents.

2 American Sociological Association. Asanet.org.

https://www.asanet.org/about/governance-and-leadership/council/presidents/edward-ross

3 The Passing of the Great Race. *Science* 25 Oct 1918: Vol. 48, Issue 1243, pp. 419-420.

https://science.sciencemag.org/content/48/1243/419

4 eugenicsarchive.ca.

http://eugenicsarchive.ca/discover/connections/53eea903803
401daea000001

5 What Happens When a Slogan Becomes the Curriculum. Conor
Friedersdorf. 3.14.2021. theatlantic.com

https://www.theatlantic.com/ideas/archive/2021/03/should-
black-lives-matter-agenda-be-taught-school/618277/

6 Whiteness is a Pandemic. Damon Young. 3.17.2021.
theroot.com

https://verysmartbrothas.theroot.com/whiteness-is-a-
pandemic-1846494770

7 Monnica T. Williams. What is Whiteness? 6.13.2020.
psychologytoday.com.

https://www.psychologytoday.com/us/blog/culturally-
speaking/202006/what-is-whiteness

8 https://blacklivesmatter.com/what-matters-ep-4-black-lives-
matters-south-bend-members-community-organizers/

9 http://www.blacklivesmattersyllabus.com/2021-classroom-
dialogue-with-deray-mckesson/

10 White Fragility. Robin Diangelo. Page 11.

11 The Oxford Companion to American Military History. Edited
by John W Chambers. 2004. oxfordreference.com

https://www.oxfordreference.com/view/10.1093/acref/9780195
071986.001.0001/acref-9780195071986-e-0618

12 Why do Asian Americans academically outperform Whites? –
The cultural explanation revisited. Social Science Research
Volume 58, July 2016, Pages 210-226. Airan Liu.

https://www.sciencedirect.com/science/article/abs/pii/S00490
89X15300570

13 Explaining Asian Americans' academic advantage over whites. Amy Hsin, Yu Xie. PNAS June 10, 2014 111 (23) 8416-8421; first published May 5, 2014

https://www.pnas.org/content/111/23/8416

12 / 14 How Americans see the state of race relations. Juliana M Horowitz, Anna Brown, Kiana Cox. Pew Research Center. Social & Demographic Trends. 4.9.2019.

https://www.pewresearch.org/social-trends/2019/04/09/how-americans-see-the-state-of-race-relations/

13 /15 news.gallop.com

https://news.gallup.com/poll/1687/race-relations.aspx

14 The reasons for geographic and racial differences in stroke study.
International Journal of Stroke. 8.26.2015. O'Neal, Judd, et al.

https://pubmed.ncbi.nlm.nih.gov/26306564/

17 Poll Finds Most in U.S. Hold Dim View of Race Relations. Kevin Sack, Megan Thee-Brenan. 7.23.2015. nytimes.com.

https://www.nytimes.com/2015/07/24/us/poll-shows-most-americans-think-race-relations-are-bad.html?auth=login-email&login=email

18 Negative View of U.S. Race Relations Grows, Poll Finds. Dalia Sussman. 5.4.2015. nytimes.com.

https://www.nytimes.com/2015/05/05/us/negative-view-of-us-race-relations-grows-poll-finds.html

19 What are Trump's #BannedWords and why do they matter? Raceforward.com

https://www.raceforward.org/bannedwords

20 Nearly half of American sports fans changed viewing habits because of social justice. Jay Busbee. 3.29.2021. sports.yahoo.com.

https://www.yahoo.com/sports/nearly-half-of-americans-changed-sports-viewing-habits-because-of-social-justice-192601834.html

CHAPTER 2. THE FRAGILE LOGIC BEHIND WHITE FRAGILITY.

1 Intellectuals and Race. Thomas Sowell. 2013. Page 51.

2 Thomas Jefferson. Notes on the State of Virginia. Electronic Edition. First edition, 2006. ca. 556K. University Library, UNC-Chapel Hill. University of North Carolina at Chapel Hill, 2006.

https://docsouth.unc.edu/southlit/jefferson/jefferson.html

3 Architects of Ruin. Peter Schweizer. 2010. Page 71.

CHAPTER 3. THE WOMAN WHO WOULD ASSASSINATE ABRAHAM LINCOLN. THE 1619 PROJECT.

1 https://www.scribd.com/document/466921269/NYT-s-1619-Project-Founder-Calls-White-Race-Barbaric-Devils-Bloodsuckers-No-Different-Than-Hitler-x

2 East Africa's forgotten slave trade. Silja Frohlich. 8.22.2019. dw.com.

https://www.dw.com/en/east-africas-forgotten-slave-trade/a-50126759

3 Recalling Africa's harrowing tale of its first slavers – The Arabs – as UK Slave Trade Abolition is commemorated. George Pavlu. 3.27.2018. newafrica.com

https://newafricanmagazine.com/16616/

4 Africa is again the world's epicenter of modern-day slavery. Abdi L Dahir. 7.23.2018. qz.com.

https://qz.com/africa/1333946/global-slavery-index-africa-has-the-highest-rate-of-modern-day-slavery-in-the-world/

5 Global Findings. Globalslaveryindex.com.

https://www.globalslaveryindex.org/2018/findings/global-findings/

6 They Said We Were Slaves. Sexual Violence by Armed Groups in the Central African Republic. Smita Sharma. 10.5.2017. hrw.org.

https://www.hrw.org/report/2017/10/05/they-said-we-are-their-slaves/sexual-violence-armed-groups-central-african

CHAPTER 4. ERIC GARNER.

1 Sharpton urges Ferguson protesters not to aid 'smear campaign' by rioting. Lauren Gambino. 8.16.2014. theguardian.com

https://www.theguardian.com/world/2014/aug/16/sharpton-ferguson-protesters-smear-campaign-rioting

2 Statement by Attorney General Holder on Federal Investigation Into Death of Eric Garner. 12.3.2014. justice.gov.

https://www.justice.gov/opa/speech/statement-attorney-general-holder-federal-investigation-death-eric-garner

3 President Obama Delivers a Statement on the Grand Jury Decision in the Death of Eric Garner. Tayna Somanader. 12.3.2014.

https://obamawhitehouse.archives.gov/blog/2014/12/03/presid
ent-obama-delivers-statement-grand-jury-decision-death-eric-
garner

4 White Teachers, Institutional Cultural Narratives, & Beliefs
about African Americans. Laurel Puchner & Linda Markowitz.
Multicultural Education. Fall, 2015.

https://files.eric.ed.gov/fulltext/EJ1090572.pdf

5 Statement by United States Attorney Richard P. Donoghue.
7.16.2019. justice.gov.

https://www.justice.gov/usao-edny/pr/statement-united-states-
attorney-richard-p-donoghue

CHAPTER 5. MICHAEL BROWN.

1 Department of Justice Report Regarding the Criminal
Investigation into the Shooting Death of Michael Brown by
Ferguson, Missouri Police Officer Darren Wilson. 3.4.2015.

https://www.justice.gov/sites/default/files/opa/press-
releases/attachments/2015/03/04/doj_report_on_shooting_of
_michael_brown_1.pdf

2 Statement by the President. 8.14.2014.
obamawhitehouse.archives.gov.

https://obamawhitehouse.archives.gov/the-press-
office/2014/08/14/statement-president

3 Remarks by the President at Congressional Black Caucus Awards Dinner. 9.28.2014. obamawhitehouse.archives.gov.

https://obamawhitehouse.archives.gov/the-press-office/2014/09/28/remarks-president-congressional-black-caucus-awards-dinner

CHAPTER 6. TAMIR RICE.

1 Justice Department Announces Closing of Investigation into 2014 Officer Involved Shooting in Cleveland, Ohio. 12.29.2020. justice.gov.

https://www.justice.gov/opa/pr/justice-department-announces-closing-investigation-2014-officer-involved-shooting-cleveland

2 Attorney General Holder Delivers Remarks at Press Conference on Investigation into Cleveland Division of Police. 12.4.2014. justice.gov.

https://www.justice.gov/opa/speech/attorney-general-holder-delivers-remarks-press-conference-investigation-cleveland

CHAPTER 7. BREONNA TAYLOR.

1 Breonna Taylor Investigation. Louisville-police.org.

https://louisville-police.org/751/Breonna-Taylor-Investigation

2 What Matters Ep. 2: Say Her Name — Breonna Taylor, a Conversation with Tamika Mallory and Taylor Family Attorney Lonita Baker. May 20, 2020. blacklivesmatter.com

https://blacklivesmatter.com/what-matters-ep-2-say-her-name-breonna-taylor-a-conversation-with-tamika-mallory-and-taylor-family-attorney-lonita-baker/

3 *Inside a Battle Over Race, Class and Power at Smith College.* A student said she was racially profiled while eating in a college dorm. An investigation found no evidence of bias. But the incident will not fade away. By Michael Powell. 2.24.2021. nytimes.com.

https://www.nytimes.com/2021/02/24/us/smith-college-race.html

4 Justice for Breonna Taylor. Change.org.

https://www.change.org/p/andy-beshear-justice-for-breonna-taylor

5 Kentucky AG's decision in the Breonna Taylor case is being picked apart. Here's why. Darcy Costello, Jonathan Bullington. 9.30.2020. usatoday.com.

https://www.usatoday.com/story/news/nation/2020/09/30/daniel-camerons-decision-breonna-taylor-case-being-picked-apart/3586028001/

6 Movement for Black Lives Statement on the Announcement in the Killing of Breonna Taylor. 9.23.2020. m4bl.org.

https://m4bl.org/press/breonna-taylor/

7 Kentucky Grand Jury Indicts 1 Of 3 Officers In Breonna Taylor Case. Rachael Treisman, Brakkton Booker, Vanessa Romo. 9.23.2020. npr.org.

https://www.npr.org/sections/live-updates-protests-for-racial-justice/2020/09/23/914250463/breonna-taylor-charging-decision-to-be-announced-this-afternoon-lawyer-says

8 Grand jury decision in Breonna Taylor case to be announced this afternoon. Phillip M Bailey. 9.23.2020. journal-courier.com.

https://www.courier-journal.com/story/news/local/breonna-taylor/2020/09/23/kentucky-attorney-general-announces-breonna-taylor-decision-wednesday/3502148001/

9 Breonna Taylor. We Must Not Stop Saying Her Name. Dahleen
Glanton. 3.15.2012. chicagotribune.com.

https://www.chicagotribune.com/columns/dahleen-glanton/ct-
glanton-breonna-taylor-anniversary-20210315-
zznc5h2zmzaz7itldqvkrh2fka-story.html

10 There is no epidemic of fatal police shootings against
unarmed Black Americans. Heather McDonald. 7.3.2020.
usatoday.com.

https://www.usatoday.com/story/opinion/2020/07/03/police-
black-killings-homicide-rates-race-injustice-
column/3235072001/

CHAPTER 8. ERIC LOGAN and BLACK LIVES MATTER SOUTH BEND.

1 Special Prosecutor's Report on Death of Eric Logan. Report on
the Death Investigation of Eric J Logan, Ric Hertel, Special
Prosecutor. Shane Tucker, Ryan Marshall, Rae Luhrsen.

https://www.scribd.com/document/451305531/Special-
Prosecutor-s-Report-on-Death-of-Eric-Logan

2 South Bend cop in fatal shooting did not have
body cam on, says man wouldn't drop knife.
Greg Swiercz, Christian Sheckler.
Southbendtribune.com.

https://www.southbendtribune.com/news/publicsafety/south-
bend-cop-in-fatal-shooting-did-not-have-
body/article_83d293e0-b7cf-56cc-a19e-e9ea03ff4ec4.html

3 Justified force or excessive? Clashing
narratives in South Bend police shooting of Eric
Logan. Christian Sheckler. 1.3.2021.
southbendtribune.com.

https://www.southbendtribune.com/news/publicsafety/justified
-force-or-excessive-clashing-narratives-in-south-bend-police-

shooting-of-eric-logan/article_d0413fca-4b6a-11eb-8ac5-dbbc778f677f.html

4 What Matters Ep. 4: Black Lives Matter's South Bend Members – Community Organizers. 6.2.2020. blacklivesmatter.com.

https://blacklivesmatter.com/what-matters-ep-4-black-lives-matters-south-bend-members-community-organizers/

5 South Bend's Police Chief, Close Ally of Pete Buttigieg, Promotes Officer Involved in Controversial Choking Death. Akela Lacy. 12.5.2019. theintercept.com.

theintercept.com, South Bend's Police Chief, Close Ally of Pete Buttigieg, Promotes Officer Involved in Controversial Choking Death. By Akela Lacy

6 Former South Bend cop 'justified' in Eric Logan shooting but charged for soliciting a prostitute. Christian Sheckler and Marek Mazurek. Mar 7, 2020. Southbendtribune.com.

https://www.southbendtribune.com/news/local/former-south-bend-cop-justified-in-eric-logan-shooting-but/article_8264b912-5fc0-11ea-a6fd-17e511e49140.html?utm_medium=social&utm_source=facebook_South_Bend_Tribune

CHAPTER 9. THE FALSE NARRATIVES OF BLM LOS ANGELES.

1 Officer Involved Shooting of Christoper Deandre Mitchell Torrance Police Department. 10.9.2019. da.lacounty.gov.

https://da.lacounty.gov/sites/default/files/pdf/JSID_OIS_10_2019_Mitchell.pdf

2 Boycott 24 Hour Fitness.

https://www.blmla.org/boycott-24-hour-fitness

3 Officer Involved Shooting of Albert Dorsey Los Angeles Police Department. 7.28.2020. da.lacounty.gov.

https://da.lacounty.gov/sites/default/files/pdf/JSID-OIS-07-28-2020-Dorsey.pdf

4 Officer Involved Shooting of Dennis Todd Williams-Rogers Los Angeles County Sheriff's Department. 2.21.2018. la.lacounty.gov.

https://da.lacounty.gov/sites/default/files/pdf/JSID_OIS_02_2018_Rogers.pdf

CHAPTER 10. THE FALSE NARRATIVE OF BLM CHICAGO.

1 Justice for Families. Blacklivesmatterchicago.com.

https://www.blacklivesmatterchicago.com/justice-for-families/

2 Police Involved Death Decision Memorandum. Decedent: Cleotha Mitchell. Cookcountystatesattorney.org.

https://www.cookcountystatesattorney.org/sites/default/files/files/documents/cleotha_mitchell_declination_memo.pdf

3 Police Involved Death Decision Memorandum. Decedent: Joshua Beal. Cookcountystatesattorney.org.

https://www.cookcountystatesattorney.org/sites/default/files/files/documents/joshua_beal_release_memo.pdf

4 Police Involved Death Decision Memorandum. Decedent: Lamar Harris. Cookcountystatesattorney.org.

https://www.cookcountystatesattorney.org/sites/default/files/files/documents/lamar_harris_declination_memo.pdf

5 Police Involved Death Decision Memorandum. Decedent: Lamar Harris and Bettie Jones. Cookcountystatesattorney.org.

https://www.cookcountystatesattorney.org/sites/default/files/fil es/documents/quintonio.pdf

6 Police Involved Death Decision Memorandum. Decedent: Richard Grimes. Cookcountystatesattorney.org.

https://www.cookcountystatesattorney.org/sites/default/files/fil es/documents/richard_grimes_declination_memo.pdf

7 Police Involved Death Decision Memorandum. Decedent: Thurman Reynolds. Cookcountystatesattorney.org.

https://www.cookcountystatesattorney.org/sites/default/files/fil es/documents/thurman_reynolds_declination_memo.pdf

8 Police Involved Death Decision Memorandum. Decedent: Derek Love. Cookcountystatesattorney.org.

https://www.cookcountystatesattorney.org/sites/default/files/fil es/documents/derek_love_declination_memo.pdf

9 Police Involved Death Decision Memorandum. Decedent: Pierre Loury. Cookcountystatesattorney.org.

https://www.cookcountystatesattorney.org/sites/default/files/fil es/documents/pierre_loury_declination_memo.pdf

CHAPTER 11. JACOB BLAKE.

1 Report on the Officer Involved Shooting of Jacob Blake. Michael D Gravely, District Attorney. Kenoshacounty.org

https://www.kenoshacounty.org/DocumentCenter/View/11827/ Report-on-the-Officer-Involved-Shooting-of-Jacob-Blake.

2 We need Black Lives Matter. The police who shot Jacob Blake prove it. Eugene Robinson. 8.24.2020. washingtonpost.com.

https://www.washingtonpost.com/opinions/we-need-black-lives-matter-the-police-who-shot-jacob-blake-prove-it/2020/08/24/91dcec8a-e638-11ea-bc79-834454439a44_story.html

3 Jacob Blake's shooting shows America has a long way to go in its journey toward a racial reckoning. Ray Sanchez. 9.4.2020. cnn.com.

https://www.cnn.com/2020/08/30/us/jacob-blake-shooting-one-week-later/index.html.

4 Jacob Blake's shooting shows America has a long way to go in its journey toward a racial reckoning. Ray Sanchez. September 4, 2020.

https://www.cnn.com/2020/08/30/us/jacob-blake-shooting-one-week-later/index.html

5 Black Lives Matter Global Network Responds after Wisconsin District Attorney Won't Charge Kenosha Police Officer in Jacob Blake Shooting. January 5, 2021.

https://blacklivesmatter.com/black-lives-matter-global-network-responds-after-wisconsin-district-attorney-wont-charge-kenosha-police-officer-in-jacob-blake-shooting/

12. DISCUSSION.
13. SOLUTIONS.
14. FINALLY (ALMOST)

15. THIS IS HOW IT STARTED.

What follows is the first chapter in the story I was writing that morphed into the preceding book.

CHAPTER ONE.

Professor Herman T. Jones was on the tenure track. It was close. This academic nirvana. This confirmation of his...what?

He couldn't really say 'contribution.' The last article he had co-authored, *Decolonizing Criminality: The Intersectionality of Post-Imperialist Offender Identity Dynamics in the Context of the Prevailing White Meta-Narrative,* had been well enough received. He just wasn't sure what it actually meant. He harbored a nebulous seed of doubt that had sprouted long ago. The article's success, and his own inner pangs discord over its intent, allowed another fine tendril of that creeping doubt to root itself in his mind like some tenacious, choking ivy.

And everyone else around him in The Department of Arts and Humanities always seemed so certain. His peers spoke with capital-A Authority. If they had any doubt as to the sincerity of their polysyllabic pearls of impenetrable wisdom or The Department's mission, they masked it with the skill of Shakespearean thespians.

Jones winced, then looked about to make certain no one had seen this. The classroom was still empty. The Department harshly frowned upon the word 'thespians' for the potential it had to unintentionally mis-label the listener who heard 'lesbians.' Once a word escaped your lips, no matter your intent, it belonged to the listener and their authentic experience of it. No take-backs. No do-overs. No pathetic explanations or futile appeals for mercy. One slip like that and he could kiss tenure goodbye.

194

The Department didn't explicitly ban any words. This was a University, after all, and free speech was a prime virtue. But free speech came with a high cost. An implicit speech code had settled over the campus over the last few years like some noxious, invisible, suffocating smog that caught like fishhooks in your chest and stung your eyes and made you want to scream, *Can't you feel it too?!? Throw down your phones and rip off your clothes and scream with me while we run free and naked through the grass! Ha-ha-ha-ha-ha!!!*

Jones winced again. Damn it! Was he losing it? Was he going insane? He was the only one who seemed affected by this imagined and yet oh-so-real seeming mental claustrophobia. He needed something, anything, to anchor him in reality. Jones needed one other person to inhale that smog and have it sear their nostrils and tell him it was true.

Then again, maybe insanity was a prerequisite for tenure. Maybe submitting to the madness was the key to conquering it. The Department was run by lunatics, after all. It told him the fact is, there are no facts and the truth is, there is no truth and that, reasonably speaking, there is no reason.

On that premise, they churned out their philosophical tools, their cognitive frameworks and their endless deconstructions and reconstructions. They were like busy little carpenters happily building up and tearing down the same house over and over and over until its splintered and utterly unrecognizable planks and beams joined together in only the alien angles of some monstrous Lovecraft deity. Only then, content, they smiled and invited you inside.

Jones considered that he was only a construct of their minds. He certainly could not be a construct of his own mind, for his own mind was not adequately deep enough to fathom the murky depths of their genius. He bobbed along, his head barely above the surface, while great, buoyant theories rose up from below like titanic, lumbering, incomprehensible new species of thought and revealed parts of their strange, glistening selves to him.

Perhaps he had once usefully risen from this vast pool of their knowledge to serve as a reverent observer. And how could anyone not revere them? From within the ivy-covered walls of their offices, they reclined in plush leather chairs and wielded omnipotence. Like metaphysical surgeons, they dissected the hearts and minds of the vast common rabble wandering in dim ignorance beyond the university's enlightenment and resected societal malignancies. They shattered entire, invisible, social frameworks of tyranny and then, from the smoldering rubble of the vanquished, they raised new, better, invisible social frameworks of tyranny.

And they spoke in an increasingly sophisticated dialect that Jones could no longer interpret. He recalled a conversation just a few days prior in The Department's staff lobby. A colleague had mentioned "the transparency of experience and the required univocality and provenance of its interpretation qua feminists."

Jones had nearly dropped his porcelain mug of coffee onto the marble floor upon hearing this. Then came the response.

"It tacitly underscores the hermeneutic necessity of rejecting dominant epistemic discourses in favor of subjugated knowledges."

This was casual conversation at the day's start! What staggering, humbling, polysyllabic cerebral gymnastics were possible when they really got warmed up?

The Professor rubbed the stubble on his face and ran a hand quickly through his remaining hair. He had to quit this. Pausing to contemplate his sanity only made him feel more insane. But not pausing to contemplate his sanity allowed the insane thoughts to multiply like devious gremlins in a pool. He considered pausing to not consider his insanity as a remedy, then dismissed this as impractical.

Think of tenure. Let that focus your thoughts. Once your tenured, you won't have to think at all.

Perhaps, Jones thought, he would be rewarded instead for his commitment. He'd put in the time. Seventeen years now. Over that span he'd gone from a trim, virile, late twenties, six-foot-one pillar of well-toned muscle to this drab, late forties partially bald guy with fleshy bags of cookie dough permanently strapped around his waist. And he was certain he was shorter. Maybe five-eleven now. And if not shorter, then somehow...diminished.

He believed that education was a noble pursuit.

Believed. Past tense.

But it must be like that in any profession, Jones reasoned. Medicine. Engineering. Law. There is the ideal form, the envisioned practice. And then there is the messy reality with all of the tedious Department politics and awkward, delicate dancing around his reputation.

There was a knock on the door.

Jones startled and a small squeak escaped his chest like a frightened bird. Had they come for him with a security guard and an empty cardboard box? He considered leaping out a window to escape.

Finally, he whimpered, "Who is it?"

"It's Sabastian. We spoke on the phone earlier."

Jones nearly melted into a warm, buttery pool of relief. "Yes. Come in."

Dewey Sabastian, Private Eye, entered the classroom. He looked like he'd been chiseled from squat block of limestone and then wrapped in a rumpled shirt, tie and trousers. He took a little notebook from a pocket and got right down to it.

"What is it exactly you want me to do?"

"I want you to tail me when I'm now around. See what I'm up to."

"What do you think you might be up to?" asked the investigator.

"That's just it. I don't know. I've lived with me my whole life and I'm just now beginning to suspect that I might be capable of anything. I might be a drug dealer or a human trafficker. Something like that."

"You sound like a dangerous man."

"You'd be amazed," said Jones. "I've been part of a secret, centuries old, nationwide cabal of miscreants bent on vicious domination and crushing oppression."

"If it's a secret, why are you telling me?"

"I've only slowly become aware of it myself. I had to do something. Who knows what I might have been up to while I just sat here doing nothing? I could be plotting some treasonous act of terror while we speak!"

"Relax. If you're as bad as you say you are, there will be evidence. We'll catch you."

"What if I'm operating under a false identity or an assumed name? What if I'm not even me?"

"Sounds like you've stumbled into a real rabbit hole."

"I just hope you can stop me before I really hurt someone."

"It'll cost you."

"Cost is no issue. Can you get started right away?"

The investigator nodded and tucked his little notebook into a pocket. "Consider it started."

"Whatever you find out, don't let me know when I'm around. I'm afraid I might try to eavesdrop on our conversation."

"A tricky bit of business."

"That's why I needed your help."

The investigator nodded, stood and left the room.

Jones was, he had unfortunately discovered, complicit in the mass oppression of a countless and ever-increasing number of marginalized groups. Groups that, content in obscurity, grew indignant when their newfound marginalized status came into being.

A decade prior this crime had been hidden, even to himself. Then Jones woke one day and saw that he and the damnable, invisible framework he'd unknowingly propagated had been responsible for every diseased abscess in the sensitive tissues of society. He had to atone for every malignant sore this society had suffered, was suffering and would ever suffer into the indeterminate future.

Jones at first had doubted that he, a bland and agreeable fellow who tried to agree with everything even when he didn't, could really be the villain in his own life story.

A female colleague had finally and furtively pulled him aside. "Listen Herman, while I'm technically required to hate you, I want you to know it's only a professional hate."

She went on to tell him that expressing skepticism about his new status as an ancient evil only confirmed his privileged place in the corrupt schematic he'd unconsciously built.

"What do I do?" Jones asked.

"There's nothing you can do."

"I can't just do nothing!"

"You also can't do anything."

She cast a look over her shoulder to confirm that no one had seen her speaking with him, then quickly left.

Eventually, Jones became shocked by the depths of his own depravity. Did he have multiple personalities, each hidden from the others, some of whom gleefully embarked on giddy sprees of wanton microaggressions and blatant rampages of pronoun deployment? Maybe bouts of amnesia or serial fugue states wherein he consorted with all manner of filthy perverts, jaundiced miscreants and Republicans? He'd never come to laying in a sloppy gutter or spooning a stranger some anonymous bed, so he thought not.

He decided the only way to escape this issue was to really embrace it. He went to see The Department Chair with a bold scheme.

"White Apologetics101? What the hell's this?" asked the Dean. She had the surly affect of a hungry bulldog stuffed into the feeble frame of a museum artifact. Jones wasn't sure of her age, but he thought she might be a million.

"It's a new course I'd like to begin teaching," said Jones.

The Chair pointed to the blank pages in the proposal. "There's nothing here under Curriculum."

"There is no curriculum."

"No curriculum?"

"No curriculum."

"How the hell can there be no curriculum?"

"A rigid curriculum is an artifact of Western methods of epistemology that needs to be rejected."

"What? I mean...yes. Of course. But how will you lead the class?"

"As the Professor, I can't lead the class. That would imply a false hierarchy of dominance and submission."

"Yes. My thinking exactly." She paused. "Who will lead the class?"

"The class will lead the class. Nothing but lived experiences and alternate voices. I might not even attend."

"That's perfect! Jones, you're really on to something here." The Chair paused and her wrinkled, leathery brow furrowed so deeply that Jones thought it might crack and reveal the skull beneath. "If there's no curriculum and no clear guidance, how the hell will it be graded?"

"That's the thing. There won't be any grades."

"No grades?"

"Grade are an antiquated system of meritocracy that punish those who think outside of Western heuristics."

There was a long pause, and Jones was beginning to fear he'd gone too far. The Chair's expression was unbearably neutral. Finally, she said, "No structure. No content. No guidance. No grades."

Jones held his breath.

"Brilliant!" said the Chair. "This could..." The Chair's eyes widened and her head rose up as if pulled by a string. "This could revolutionize higher studies as we know them! A university system of learning that wholly rejects the university system of learning! And to think it germinated right here in my Department!"

Jones grinned and nodded.

The Chair scrutinized him. "Jones, I was really beginning to doubt you. But this? This could set you back on tenure track."

"That's great!" said Jones, who had not yet realized he was off the track. He maintained a plastic grin, but inside he wilted with this knowledge of his near professional demise.

"When can you have this class ready?" asked the Chair. "The new term starts in a week."

"It's ready now," said Jones. "Preparations were complete as soon as I abandoned preparations."

"Oh. Right. Of course. Well, fill it with students and keep me informed of your progress. And for now, keep this just between you and me."

In the week that followed, the class quickly filled to its capacity of twenty students. Now, sitting alone in the classroom with just minutes to spare before the first anti-lecture and lack of assignments, Jones was filled with excited dread. His career and reputation hinged on the interactions between twenty relatively inexperienced and ignorant yet profoundly opinionated young people. As their Professor, he was to be powerless against them and could hold no sway over them.

Too late to turn back, Jones gritted his teeth and committed himself to the path ahead.

They filed into the classroom silently, each navigating the tiered lecture hall, locating an empty space and sitting all without ever once taking their eyes from their phones. Had Jones tried that himself, he knew he'd have broken all of his ankles and some of his legs. Some of the students chewed gum. Some bobbed their heads to music emitted from wireless earbuds. Others sipped from steaming, fully recyclable and compostable cups of organic free trade coffee. None seemed to notice their Professor.

The man anxiously scanned the college kids before him. A few years ago, he might have tried to guess their personalities based on their appearances. The slacker who would forever be asking for extra credit. The high achiever annoyingly attending every aid session to ensure their 103% in the class didn't plummet to a 102%. The kid who would show up only on the first day and the last day and still manage a solid B. The rare bored genius who had already mastered the material and made their professors sweat each time they raised a hand in class to ask the obscure, insightful, perfect questions that then kept their mentors awake at night.

But the kids had changed.

They no longer seemed like a bunch of eager little cups, some awed, others arrogant, all begging to be filled with knowledge and experience.

Now?

Now they arrived already certain of their knowledge and only wanted their professors to confirm it. And they had all the experience they desired via an infinite stream of pixelated memes vomited forth from the omnipresent phones glued to their pale, pudgy little hands. Hands that had never known blisters or callouses. Hands that had likely never climbed a tree or swung a hammer or skipped smooth, ovoid stones across the pristine, greyish purple surface of a pond at dusk while your girlfriend, the girl you still love and regret all these years later, laughed and bumbled her first few attempts until she actually beat your record and then ran her fingers across your neck, dragged you down onto the deserted, sandy shore and cursed you with the one perfect, blissful moment in your life, the one that still wakes you up with a pang of unfulfilled longing and the cutting knowledge that it will never be equaled. Jones wanted to smack the damnable devices from their grips and shake them all by their ears and shout into their perfect, youthful faces, *Damn it! Wake up! Wake up and live! Really live before you physically and mentally atrophy into your cynical, disappointed, disillusioned future selves!*

Jones realized that he'd been murmuring these thoughts in faint, guttural tones and with clenched fists. His students all looked at him now. He froze and ceased breathing for a few prolonged seconds.

"Hello," Jones said at last.

More seconds ticked off the ancient analogue clock on the wall behind him.

"So, what?" This was Jane, a slim girl in the third row with an almond shaped face and keen eyes. "What do we do?"

"Whatever you want," Jones answered.

"What do you mean, whatever we want?" asked Ewing, a heavyset kid with a childlike face.

"I mean whatever you want. You get to set the class agenda and topics and assignments and so forth. Literally, whatever you want."

Jane looked skeptical. "Well, we need class credits in Sociology, so we need to stick to related subjects."

This provoked a few shrugs and nods.

"Every subject *is* related to Sociology," said Jones. "Money. Religion. The unintended consequences of space travel on our view of an infinite cosmos. You can point the lens of Sociology at anything - *anything* – and dream up new ways to think about it. Someone name a subject. Any subject."

"Algebra," came a voice from the crowd.

"Yes," said Jones. "Even algebra. The ceaseless rearrangements of variables and constants and unknowns. The poor and lowly engineer can only use them to build better bridges and bullets and super-absorbent diapers. But the sociologist? The sociologist can imagine them out of existence!"

Jones' heart was hammering and he felt young again. He felt thirty-six!

"Algebra. Calculous. Physics. Chemistry. Everything a man can conceive or believe or dream. All knowledge, reason, morality, religion, art and science were once obscure notions that frightened us. Then they became interwoven into a shared collective consciousness that upheld society and kept it from sinking into chaotic oblivion. Now they are all oppressive myths that a society creates in order to maintain the existing power structure of dominance and submission. Someday I hope they might be the base and superstructure of a neo-Marxist socio-sexual philosophy based on the human drive to reproduce.

Something really hot and steamy and suggestive that we can all really get behind."

Now Jones became transcendent with the limitless possibilities of negating everything. He existed not in the classroom, but in an ethereal, nihilistic joy of omnipresent nothingness.

"None of that sounds very useful," Ewing observed.

"We are on a university campus," said Jones. "We are insulated from practical applications and the tedious pragmatism of actual daily life. We are academics and intellectuals. We are the intelligentsia! We don't have to produce intelligent ideas or even good ideas. Only novel ideas. Publishable ideas that our peers will review and validate as real. Ideas that sell books. Ideas will justify our tenures and maintain our elite status."

"Even if these ideas bad for society in general?" someone asked.

"That's just it. We've already erased good and bad. Right and wrong. We've nullified morality. We've negated all facts and even the scientific method for producing them. All of these things exist only in the villainous social framework dominated maintained by prevailing groups to marginalize everyone else. And so, by using this idea to erase everything, we're free to say anything. Anything! We can wallow in gratuitous minimalism! Create ever increasing reductionist diminishments! We can reject the reality of realism as real!"

A girl named Bev spoke up. She had an inquisitive, rabbit like face with a tiny, twitching nose and he eyes that seemed to take in everything at once. "So, we just talk?"

"If that's what you want," said the Professor.

"Who decides who is right?" asked Jane.

"I think all opinions should be equal," said Ewing. "No capitalistic commandeering of thought. No hoarding of intellectual assets."

"All opinions can be equally considered," said a kid named Jack. "But all opinions can't be equal."

"That's a damn bourgeoisie lie!" said Ewing.

"That's your opinion," said Jack.

Jane spoke up. "Opinions are just derivatives of our experiences within false social structures. There's no way to quantify differences between them."

Bev was impressed. "Is that a fact?"

"Of course." Jane never doubted anything she said because, to her knowledge, she had never been wrong.

In her own mind, Jane was a true crusader for social justice, even though she'd never really paused to considered what 'justice' meant. There was no time to pause and no need to consider. Rampant injustice was omnipresent. It was, figuratively speaking, in the very literal DNA of American society and literally lurked in every figure of speech. And if injustice was never idle, then she couldn't be either.

Take even the simplest act in modern society, and Jane could point out the latent oppression festering within. Ordering a cup of coffee signified the shameful past colonial practices of dominating indigenous groups and appropriating their steaming hot beverages of choice. Getting dressed every day entailed putting on at least one cotton garment, cotton representing the prior enslavement of millions. Simply crossing a city street at the crosswalk meant that you understood and had become almost unconscious of your place in White, Western civic society. Jane, therefore, only crossed streets in the middle of the block, Starbucks in hand, denim jeans fitting just right, and she was faintly perturbed that no one had noted this act of rebellion.

Jane kept herself busy zipping across the country to attend protests, vigils and rallies via Facetime from her living room while discovering social justice memes, liking social justice memes and forwarding social justice memes. She and everyone she knew were equally committed to the cause.

It often shocked Jane that not everyone was as shocked as she was. Every day in America immigrants were being detained at the US border while their only crime was breaking US law. Every day peaceful social justice protestors were being tear gassed and arrested for violently defacing and burning Federal property. Every day in America some transgender high school girl was not allowed to shower naked with her prim, conservative classmates who were too phobic to appreciate the feminine beauty of her penis, testes and testosterone drenched bone structure and musculature. It made no sense.

In every conversation, Jane was hypervigilant for any trace of racism, sexism, toxic masculinity, homophobia, transphobia, fat shaming, misgendering, appropriation, implicit bias or hate speech. It was exhausting and often required dissecting the speaker's actual words to reveal their true malignant intent, but

209

like a seasoned surgeon, Jane possessed the stamina and skill required. Unlike a true surgeon, few of Jane's subjects ever thanked her for diagnosing their cancerous thoughts.

In fact, she was always scouring society for unexplored or identified offenses. She considered the real consequences of nano-aggressions such White artists appropriating black paint into their pallets or segregating it out altogether. She intended to coin the concept of "rape speech," the verbal assault on an unwilling, unconsenting listener that attempts to penetrate the listener's mind with unwanted ideas, potentially impregnating the listener's psyche with ideas that might germinate into actionable intent contrary to Progressive ideology.

Jane was glad to live in an age when educators and philosophers had reached the final, ultimate truth. A grand, unsurpassable, infallible truth that surpassed all previous theories, each of which had themselves surpassed previous theories. Jane wondered if Sociology and Philosophy would cease to exist as subjects of study since her generation had solved all their conundrums.

She had no sympathy for the countless generations prior that suffered through the muddled ignorance of faulty and inferior thinkers like Plato, Nietzsche and Machiavelli. It was more of a condescending pity. Jane's generation did not stand on the shoulders of such intellectual giants, they slayed them and stood over their ignorant corpses, confident and proud to wield their ultimate truth like a weapon when needed.

Jane cheered those who vandalized and toppled the statues of old heroes and smashed the windows of museums. She supported those who burned police precincts and occupied city blocks and shattered storefronts. She applauded those who set fire to Federal buildings while assaulting police with bricks and bats and bombs. This was truth in action. This was progressive social justice in its truest and inevitable form. Future generations, Jane was sure, would be forever grateful for these glorious acts of liberation that, while technically illegal and nearly indistinguishable from prison riots, were surely justifiable in the name of toppling White Centrism in all of its invisible, onerous forms.

Despite the lofty, unassailable tower of truth and tolerance Jane stood upon there were still those with the arrogant audacity to question, doubt and oppose her.